Tea Basics

Tea Basics

A Quick and Easy Guide

Wendy Rasmussen
Ric Rhinehart

JOHN WILEY & SONS, INC.
New York / Chichester / Weinheim / Brisbane / Singapore / Toronto

This book is printed on acid-free paper. ♾

Published by John Wiley & Sons, Inc.

Published simultaneously in Canada.

Library of Congress Cataloging-in-Publication Data:

Rasmussen, Wendy (Wendy S.)
Tea basics : a quick and easy guide/ Wendy Rasmussen and Ric Rhinehart.
p. c.m.
Includes bibliographical references and index.
ISBN 0-471-18518-3 (pbk. : alk. paper)
1. Tea. I. Rhinehart, Ric. II. Title.
TX817.T3R37 1998
641.3'372—dc21 98-28198

Printed in the United States of America

10 9 8 7 6 5 4 3 2 1

CONTENTS

PREFACE

This book is meant to introduce you to the rich and rewarding world of tea. Not just any old tea, certainly not those tea bags you purchased off the grocery store shelf in 1974, still sitting in the back of the pantry. No, this is the world of Premium Tea.

How are we going to introduce you? What defines the ultimate cup of tea? The truth is, you will get a thousand answers from every thousand people you ask.

So, how do we define our industry or the products they manufacture within the framework of "premium or specialty?" There isn't a simple answer, because tea is rarely a simple beverage; it is complex and ever changing. To conscientiously define *premium,* we would have to change the answer every year, because teas change every year and new products emerge under the auspices of "tea."

To define *premium* for this industry, we would have to look at what tea has been, and what it currently is, without ever being able to predict what it will be. Most of us don't think about it, but tea is an agricultural commodity. The cup of tea you enjoy iced with lemon, or steaming hot in delicate china cups, is the product of a bush! As such, it is subject to the whims of nature and, worse yet, the sometimes terrible whims of man. Floods, insects, and warfare impact the world of tea.

But, even if we *could* define *premium* and knew, for example, that the Darjeeling standards we set up as premium would remain constant in next year's crop, those standards would not define premium for every taster. Taste is a personal and subjective experience. So, while we avoid defining the term *premium* in any objective sense (there is no chemical analysis we know of that defines a premium tea), we will strive to provide you with the tools necessary to define what makes the ultimate cup of tea for yourself.

Learning to cup tea, finding out how it is grown and processed, establishing the fundamentals of blending, storing, and brewing are all important and necessary elements for the dedicated consumer who wants a great "cuppa," but what you will discover is that the best tea for you personally will change on a seasonal, daily, or maybe even hourly basis. Your favorite tea for a summertime thirst-quenching iced beverage isn't necessarily the best tea for curling up with a good book in front of the fire. What we hope is that, after reading this book, you will begin to *think* about what makes up the best tea whether you are enjoying tea in tea bags, loose leaf, ready-to-drink, or teas blended with flavoring oils and/or herbal components.

Finally, we want to introduce you to the concept

of classic varietal teas that have been established for hundreds of years but today are increasingly rare commodities. Learning to appreciate tea as a product solely of careful plant management, to discover subtle taste characteristics derived from origin, not from flavoring oils or other additives—this is a fantastic adventure no tea lover should miss. In a marketplace where tea drinkers are enjoying the likes of "caramel pear" black tea, it may not be the most popular or profitable side of tea, but it is well worth your time and effort.

You—and similarly minded souls—taking this adventure seriously is also the only chance our industry has of retaining the traditional standards for varietal teas. So, we won't argue that some flavored teas are indeed better than others, either through skillful product development and/or use of better materials, but take your tastebuds beyond this and discover what premium means within the framework of naturally occurring tea flavors. By educating you about what tea has to offer in and of itself, we hope to support the growers who create these unique flavors and ensure that the traditional orthodox manufacture of tea is preserved.

As a final note, we have tried to touch on as many relevant areas as possible within the parameters of a single slim volume. Each chapter in this book could reasonably be expanded to fill an entire text on its own. This is one of the beauties of tea. Just as there are teas to satisfy any taste, the study of tea can also present areas of interest to anyone from historians to chemists, storytellers to venture capitalists (well, these two might be closer than we think). Anyway, we hope you enjoy the little sips we have presented here, find them useful and informative, and, perhaps, are even inspired to further your own education by the cupful!

ACKNOWLEDGMENTS

Although while writing a concise book on such a broad subject is definitely a challenge, the greater challenge is keeping the acknowledgements section brief given the number of people who have shared their time, knowledge and passion with us.

The greatest debt of all is to Mr. Michael Spillane of G. S. Haly. Over ten years ago, Wendy had the extreme luck of landing a job with Castle Communications (we'll get to that debt in a minute). One of the more enjoyable aspects of this job was producing a little newsletter called *The Tea Quarterly* and writing about tea for various trade publications. The man who always returned phone calls, answered every stupid question ever asked about tea, and then gave critical insight into tasting them is Mike Spillane. For Ric, the G. S. Haly Company was instrumental in creating a tea lover out of a dedicated coffee man. He has continued to be badgered by both of us (nearly incessantly) since then, and he is still the greatest and most patient teacher in the world of tea.

Second only to Mr. Spillane is our mentor and friend, Mr. Tim Castle. He helped us learn how to taste and put the experience into words. This may be the most difficult skill in the world to pass on to another person, but as one of the most astute and poetic people we know, he does a fine job. He also put up with Wendy as an employee for close to a decade, only firing her occasionally, although she probably deserved it more often. These two built the foundation of our combined passion for and knowledge about tea, and they served unwittingly as our introduction to one another, although we won't make them take responsibility for either one.

Now, to all the people who helped on this particular endeavor, and they are many! Kevin Knox and Julie Sheldon Huffaker for blazing the trail for us with their fantastic *Coffee Basics.* Mr. Shashank Goel of Ambootia who listened to us patiently, introduced us to tea from a grower's perspective, and provided us with all of the photos for this book. Ms. Susan Vendeland of Illahe Hills Tea Farm for her invaluable research into tea and health. Ms. Dorothea Johnson of the Washington School of Protocol for all things etiquette. Ms. Martha Widmann for her wonderful drawings. All the patient readers, fact checkers, and style police, including Mr. Bruce Mullins of Xanadu (Coffee Bean International) and Mr. Ashok Kumar of Goomtee.

There are also some people who need to be thanked, not because they are tea fanatics (or even tea drinkers, shame on them) but because they have provided a network of support without which we never could have written this book. Thanks to our parents,

David and Kathy Rasmussen and Bill and Jean Rhinehart. Thank you to the entire Santa Gertrudes Gang: the Kellys, the Kinions, the Sheppards, the Mullins, the Wilsons, the Ericksons, and, especially, our best friends and second family—Rob, JoLynn, Molly, Nolan, and Meggie Glisson.

Finally, a big thank you to our patient, inspiring, smart, and wonderful kids—Patrick, Alex, Henry and Annie, tea drinkers all!

Wendy Rasmussen
Ric Rhinehart

Tea Basics

What Is Tea?

In colloquial English, the word *tea* has a broad variety of definitions and uses. It may refer to a beverage that is made by steeping the processed leaves of the plant *Camellia sinensis* in hot water, it may refer to those leaves in their dry form, it can describe almost any beverage made in a similar fashion from botanical ingredients, or for a mixture of dry botanical ingredients. In addition, tea may refer to the ceremonial service of hot beverages, sometimes accompanied by a light meal. This book focuses on the first, and, to some degree, second definitions of the word.

The One True Leaf: *Camellia sinensis*

When we refer to tea, we are talking about the dried, processed leaves of a single plant, the *Camellia sinensis*. The tea plant is an evergreen, perennial shrub of the genus *Camellia*, which thrives in subtropic and highland tropic regions. *Camellia sinensis* is one of over 82 species in the genus *Camellia*. Gardeners and landscapers are very familiar with its cousin, the *Camellia japonica*, which is often planted in North America as an evergreen hedge in areas that are free of killing frosts. The tea plant is very similar in appearance to this ornamental plant, and can be cultivated in most frost-free regions as an interesting addition to the garden (see Fig. 1.1). There are four varieties of the tea plant which are cultivated commercially: the China types, Assam (India) types, Hybrid types (a cross of China and Assam types), and Cambodia types.

The China, Assam, and hybrid types, or *jats*, as they are called, are the major commercial cultivars. (*Jat* is an Assamese word that refers to the provenance of a tea plant.) The China jat is the tea bush that produced the first teas which were embraced by the Chinese over 1200 years ago, and much later by most of the western world. This type of tea bush is generally short in stature, with relatively small leaves, grows well at higher altitudes, and is fairly cold tolerant, and quite hardy. The Assam jat is relatively taller than the

Figure 1.1 Two leaves and a bud, the classic topmost portion of new growth that is plucked for fine tea (© Ambootia, Photographer: James Prinz, Chicago)

China jat, with larger leaves and considerably less cold tolerance, making it best suited for cultivation in lower, warmer climates. Hybrid types, as might be expected, are generally somewhere between the two in stature, leaf size, and cold tolerance.

In one of tea's many odd historical points, the Assam jat, which is indigenous to India, was the center of some dispute amongst nineteenth century English botanists, who encountered it growing wild in some remote regions of India but were convinced that it was not a tea plant because it was different from the Chinese plant they were familiar with. Early pioneers of tea cultivation in India went so far as to import

China seed and plant it in India, where it failed to perform very well because of the climate. It was eventually replaced by the naturally occurring Assam jat, which, along with many hybrids, is the standard cultivar throughout India and Sri Lanka today.

Regardless of the variety and heritage of the plant from which it is harvested, all true teas are made exclusively from the young leaves, buds, and internodes, or two leaves and a bud, of this single species of *Camellia*. They are processed in a wide variety of traditional as well as modern methods to yield the vast spectrum of green, oolong, and black teas that are available in today's commercial markets.

A Checklist: What Is Fine Tea?

1. An honest tea, one whose components are what they claim to be, for example, First Flush Darjeeling, a tea harvested at first flush from a recognized garden in the Darjeeling district of northern India.

2. A recognizable tea, one whose taste and aroma match its name. If it is a varietal tea it will have the taste characteristics typical of its origin, for example, a Fanciest Formosa Oolong, which has a sweet, dry, floral, peach-

pit character. For flavored teas, a blackberry tea will have the aroma of fresh blackberries, and a slightly citric tang in its flavor.

3. A tea with credentials, for example, if it is an organic product, it can provide certification; if it is a blend of herbal and black tea, then the producer knows the origin and grade of black tea and where the herbal component was grown; if it is flavored, the manufacturer can tell you what type of oil was used—natural, nature-identic, and so on—as well as what was used for the base tea.
4. A tea that meets your criteria of premium; it tastes great to you!

Tea's Place in the World

Tea, the beverage, is the second most widely consumed drink in world, exceeded only by the most necessary of all liquids, water. Commercial production of tea occurs in some forty countries around the world, yielding an annual total of about 2.7 million metric tons, or nearly 6 billion pounds (see Figure 1.2)! This translates loosely to 1.9 trillion cups of tea consumed annually!

Who is drinking all this tea? Well, the highest per capita consumption in the world happens on the Em-

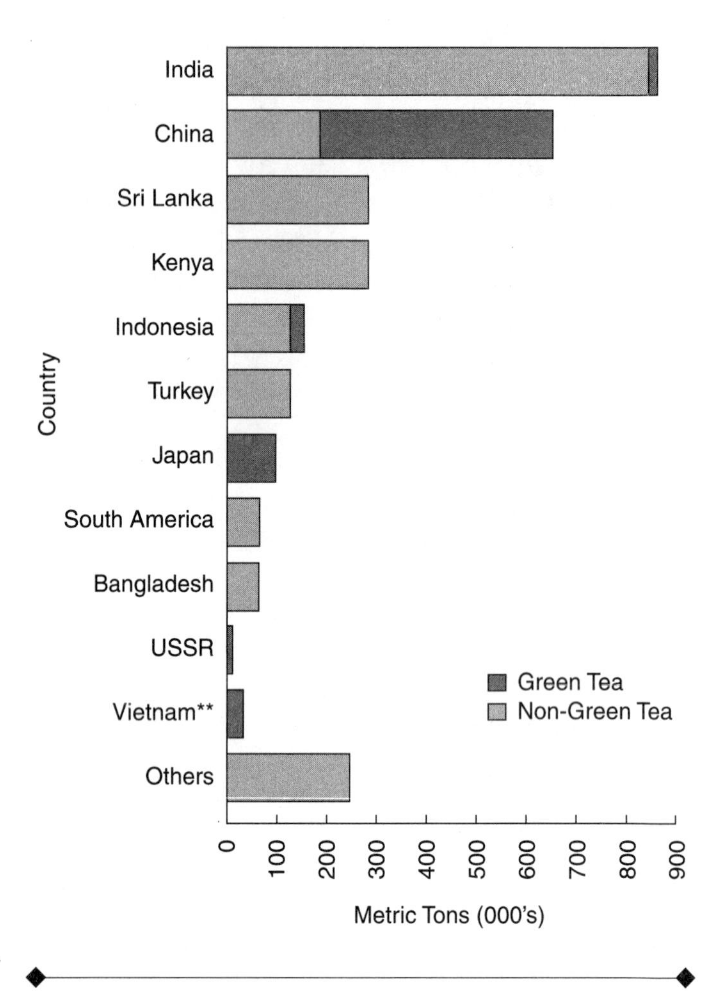

Figure 1.2 Chart of worldwide tea production (Source: *USDA*)

erald Isle: The Irish consume some 3.83 cups per person per day. The next most active consumers are the Kuwaitis, at 3.21 cups per day. Americans rank near the bottom worldwide, quaffing less than half a cup per day, most of that in the form of iced tea (see Fig. 1.3).

Tea is a significant economic force in most of the countries in which it is cultivated. In India, for example, it accounts for 1 percent of all exports, notwithstanding the fact that India consumes the lion's share of its production internally. It is difficult to translate the entire tea trade into a dollar figure, but estimates for the U.S. tea trade are approximately $4.4 billion, one of the smaller fragments of the world market for tea.

Creating a True Specialty: Commercial Versus Fine Teas

Tea is in the strictest sense an agricultural product. The distinction between commercial grades of tea and truly exceptional tea begins on the farm or tea garden, and continues through every stage of processing and handling, including brewing. At every step of the way, attention to detail and passionate care for the end result contribute to the final quality of the cup. The producer of commercial grades is primarily concerned with yield—what is the most cost-effective method of producing the maximum amount of sale-

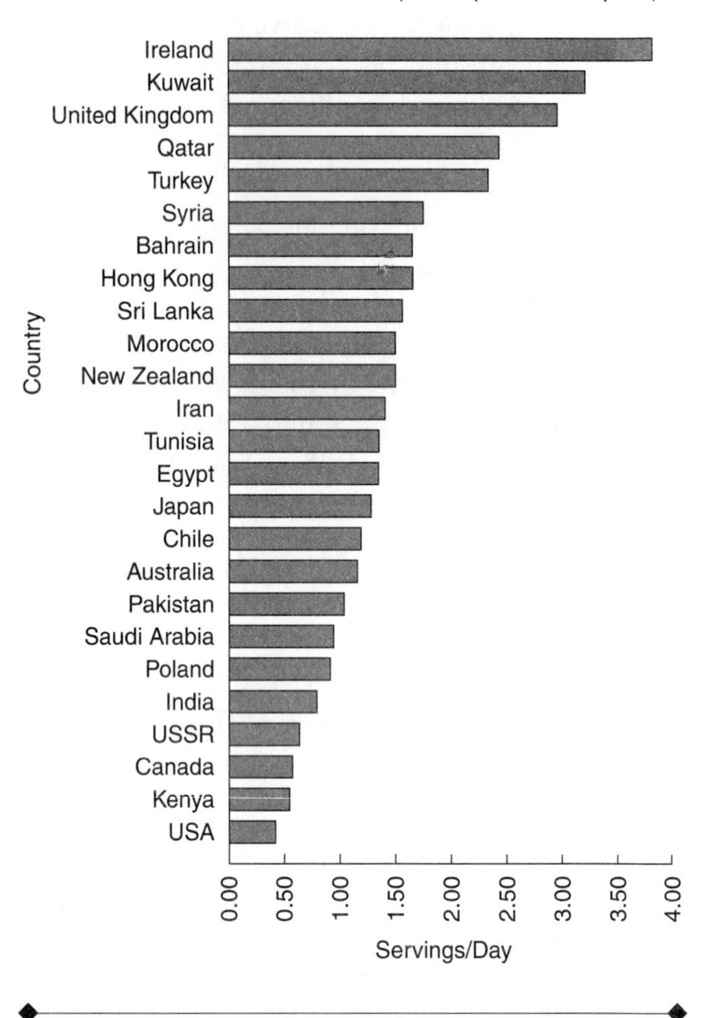

Figure 1.3 Who drinks the most tea? (Source: USDA)

able tea. The true specialty or premium tea producer is concerned first and foremost with the quality of his product, and is influenced by tradition, the desire for the exceptional, a love of tea, and a sense of pride in his product. This is not to say that economics are not a factor, but the product-driven specialty producer hopes to recoup the time, energy, and money he puts into creating a premium product by selling it for a higher price, not by merely having more to sell as a commodity.

Cultivation and Harvesting: Beyond Two Leaves and a Bud

Tea as an agricultural crop has some fairly specific requirements in terms of maximum and minimum temperatures, soil chemistry, available moisture, and so on. Hybrids of China and Assam jat are frequently used as the plant of choice in much of the world, and are selected to thrive in the area where the tea garden or farm is located. New bushes are typically grown through vegetative propagation, that is, cuttings from the best plants, known as *mother bushes*, are rooted and then planted out (see Fig. 1.4). Careful selection for taste rather than yield, resistance to disease, or increased hardiness is the hallmark of the specialty producer at this stage.

Tea left to its own devices will grow into a fairly substantial tree, and on the farms we are most familiar with there are always some tea bushes allowed to do so for the purpose of growing seeds. For tea pro-

Figure 1.4 A young clonal plant which is ready to leave the nursery and be planted out in the garden (© Ambootia, Photographer: James Prinz, Chicago)

duction, however, it is necessary to train the tea plants into bushes, and great care is taken to create a shape which lends itself to consistent picking, or plucking. This process, called *bringing into bearing*, or *frame formation,* is achieved through pruning and, in some cases, pegging. *Pegging* is the practice of bending some branches down and pegging them into position. The relatively flat, consistent surface of the trained tea bushes is known as the *plucking table*. Repeated plucking of the new growth on the plucking table eventually results in a growing surface that is heavily congested by old stems, and these must be cut out periodically, either by *skiffing*, a cut at only the highest levels, which allows new growth and thus new plucking to return quickly, or by *maintenance pruning*, a deeper cut, which also has the effect of lowering the plucking table down to a convenient height for the people doing the plucking. Maintenance pruning is generally followed by tipping. *Tipping* involves leaving four to six inches of stem and plucking over it. This process increases the number of branches which will produce fresh points for plucking and helps to produce a flat table for plucking.

Beyond propagation and pruning, all the usual farming practices associated with commercial crops are important for tea production. Weeds and pests must be controlled, and fertilizers, either chemical or organic, must be applied. Tea is a labor-and attention-intensive crop, requiring tremendous human effort at every stage from soil preparation to plucking.

Harvesting, or plucking, is done by hand for all

truly specialty or premium grade teas, with the notable exception of Japan, where shears are used. The best teas are made from the youngest shoots of the plant, and pluckers are taught to be very selective (see Fig. 1.5). Two leaves and a bud constitutes a fine plucking, more than this is a coarse plucking. A practiced plucker on a lower-grown or level estate can pluck about 90,000 shoots a day, which will yield about 27 pounds of finished, or *made*, tea. In more mountainous areas, such as the Darjeeling district of India, pluckers average about 30,000 shoots in a day. Not surprisingly, on tea estates where plucking is done by hand, up to 80 percent of the labor force will be employed as pluckers.

Figure 1.5 A skilled plucker in the Darjeeling region of India carefully picks the top two leaves and a bud. (© Ambootia, Photographer: James Prinz, Chicago)

The freshly plucked tea must be carefully handled. If it is piled too high in the baskets used to collect it, the leaves at the bottom will be crushed, and bacterial development can begin, potentially harming quality. Generally, the fresh-plucked leaves are transported immediately to the factory, where processing begins, and the tea is on its way to becoming green, oolong, or black tea (see Fig. 1.6).

PROCESSING

The type of tea that will be produced from the freshly plucked leaves is driven mainly by tradition and ge-

Figure 1.6 Freshly plucked tea is brought to the factory area where it is weighed before processing begins. (© Ambootia, Photographer: James Prinz, Chicago)

ography. It is possible to make any of the three common forms of tea from any tea plant in any region, but most tea producers have long standing commitments to one process or another, and, in general, all the farming practices and plant selections have converged to produce a single style in any given estate or geography. India and Ceylon, for example, produce almost exclusively black teas, while Formosa favors Oolong, and Japan forsakes all other processes for green tea. The processing alone will determine what type of tea is produced.

Green Tea Processing

Green tea, as one would suppose, is the least processed of all tea types. The freshly plucked leaves are steamed or pan fired to halt active enzymes, which cause fermentation, or oxidation. This causes the leaves to be soft and pliable. They are then generally rolled into some traditional shape, ranging from tiny pellets (gunpowder) to long, wiry strands (Sencha), and just about any shape in between. Rolling may also be the first step of drying the tea, as in the case of most Japanese green tea manufacture. Additional drying is accomplished through continued rolling, pan firing, or other heat processes until the tea reaches its final stage of less than 4 percent moisture. There are hundreds of types of green tea, achieved by varying the style of firing, as well as the style of rolling and drying. Most are defined to some degree by how they are fired, broadly classed as either steam fired or pan-fired teas.

Black Tea Processing

Black tea processing is considerably more complex. The freshly plucked leaves are brought to the tea factory, which is most often located on the estate, or very near to a collection of small farms. Once it arrives, the tea is laid out on screens fitted to long wooden boxes called withering troughs. Here the tea is allowed to *wither*, a process very much what it sounds like: Literally, air passing through and over the intact leaves begins to remove moisture. The rate at which air passes through the leaves, the temperature of the air, and even the depth of the tea piled in the troughs will impact the final quality of the tea. For great tea, tremendous care must be taken at this stage. How dry the tea is allowed to become is determined by what process will be used to make the black tea from this stage. In general, there are two available processes—orthodox manufacture and CTC (for crush, tear, and curl), a more highly mechanized process primarily used for the production of tea-bag grades.

The withered tea, reduced to about 60 percent moisture content, is then rolled, usually by mechanical rollers, although this can be accomplished by hand (see Fig. 1.7). This rolling disrupts the cellular structure of the tea leaves, releasing oxidase enzymes present in the leaf that will combine with polyphenols and other constituents in the leaf to form the unique molecular structures which give black tea its distinctive flavor and aroma.

From the orthodox roller, the processed leaves will pass through vibrating sifters that take out and

Figure 1.7 Orthodox rolling machines in an Indian tea factory. The gentle rolling of the tea will leave them largely intact for better leaf grades.
(© Ambootia, Photographer: James Prinz, Chicago)

separate clumps or balls of wet, crushed tea leaves, and then move on to the fermentation stage (see Fig. 1.8). Fermentation is actually the oxidation of the tea constituents. Chemical interaction between the various components of the tea leaf in the presence of oxygen will cause the tea to turn from a green to a coppery red to deep brown and, finally, a nearly black color. The length of time and degree of oxidation will determine the final flavor and aroma characteristics of the tea.

After fermentation, the tea is dried, or fired, using air that has been heated to between 210 and 250 de-

Figure 1.8 The tea is now ready for fermentation, the critical stage which will determine the final taste characteristics. (© Ambootia, Photographer: James Prinz, Chicago)

grees Fahrenheit (see Fig. 1.9). The moisture content is reduced to around 3%, the tea is then sifted into various sizes, and the stalk and fiber are removed. Sifting is accomplished by a variety of sieves, each succeeding one finer than the previous; the pieces which do not pass through any given sieve are conveyed to a designated container. This is the rough grading of the leaf, which will determine whether it is a leaf grade or one of many smaller broken grades (see Fig. 1.10). Stems, stalk, and fiber are removed by passing the tea over or under electrostatically charged rollers prior to entering the sieves. The charged rollers attract the fibers, which are then brushed off and col-

Figure 1.9 The oxidized tea must be carefully dried to stop any additional fermentation and reduce the moisture content to shelf stable levels.
(© Ambootia, Photographer: James Prinz, Chicago)

lected. The final step in processing is tasting the tea for quality control (see Fig. 1.11).

Oolong Processing

Oolong, or semifermented tea, is processed in a similar fashion to black tea. The freshly plucked leaves are spread out thinly (usually on a flat bamboo basket), and withered in the sun for about 30 to 60 minutes. This process is called *Sai Qing,* and the length of time it continues is determined by the weather and available sunlight. After Sai Qing, the tea is transferred indoors and withered at room temperature. This process, called *Lang Qing,* continues for

Figure 1.10 Machine sifting and hand sifting are both employed to separate the made tea by leaf size. (© Ambootia, Photographer: James Prinz, Chicago)

six to eight hours, with the leaves being gently stirred by hand every hour or so. Some fermentation begins to take place during this process, and the unique and delightful flavor of Oolong tea begins here. The next step, *Sha Qing*, involves pan firing to kill the oxidase enzymes and stop any fermentation. After pan firing, the leaves go through four more processes: *Rou Jian*, or rolling; *Mao Huo*, second firing; *Liang Che*, cold rolling; and *Zu Huo*, final firing.

Scented Teas

Tea has a long and illustrious history of being combined with other botanical ingredients to create

Figure 1.11 The plantation manager and quality control staff taste and assess every tea made.
(© Ambootia, Photographer: James Prinz, Chicago)

unique flavors and aromas. The dried tea leaf is highly receptive to absorbing volatile oils, compounds, or any other flavor components with which it comes in contact. (This is very important to remember when storing tea, as leaving it exposed to strong scents will almost certainly affect it.) The early Chinese were known to scent tea with such delicacies as onions and garlic. Other scenting agents have withstood the test of time to become classics. Jasmine flowers, lychee fruit, rose petals, and orchids have all come to be recognized standards of scented tea.

Scenting is generally accomplished by the direct introduction of the scenting agent to the dried tea leaf. Any style of tea can be scented, although green and black teas are most commonly used. One of the more stellar exceptions to this is Jasmine tea, which is traditionally based in Pouchong tea, a very lightly fermented Oolong style. Green tea is also used as a jasmine base, but the most highly regarded standards are all made with Pouchong leaf. In this process, the unopened blossoms of night-blooming jasmine are layered on the tea and enclosed. The blossoms pop open, releasing their heady aroma, which is imparted to the tea leaves. The spent blossoms are removed, and fresh unopened blooms are added, allowed to open, and removed. This process may continue up to twelve times in top grades.

Regardless of the type of tea produced, or the type of process used, tremendous care and attention to detail at every step of the process must be taken, or the resulting tea will fail to become a truly special tea.

AUCTIONS AND PRIVATE SALES: THE LONG JOURNEY FROM FIELD TO CUP

Once it has been processed, graded, and packed, tea begins its journey into the world market. How and where it is sold is largely determined by the country of origin. Prior to World War II, much of the world's tea supply was sold at auction in London. After the war, with many former colonies gaining independence, the London auctions gradually began to decline in importance, until they finally ceased altogether in 1998.

In modern times, a great deal of tea is sold at public auctions in commercial centers of the origin countries. Indian tea is sold at auction in Calcutta, Guwahati, Siliguri, and Cochin. Sales are transacted in Indian rupees, and prices are widely affected by currency exchange rates. Ceylon tea is similarly sold at auction in Colombo, again in local currency, the Sri Lankan rupee. Other important auctions take place in Mombassa, Kenya; Limbe, Malawi; and Jakarta, Indonesia. The Jakarta auctions have the distinction of being the only auctions where tea is sold in U.S. dollars.

China teas are ostensibly sold only by the official state agency, a bureaucracy known as China National Native Produce and Animal By-product Import and Export Corporation. This multitentacled bureaucracy did an excellent job of standardizing the wide-ranging styles and types of teas produced in the various provinces and, until recently, the tea standards were very consistent. Lately, privatization and an increasing tendency towards capitalism have opened a variety of gray-market sources. This has, unfortunately, negatively impacted the consistency of the established standards.

Apart from the auction systems, most other tea is sold in private deals between growers and exporters, brokers, or other buyers. The exporters, in turn, generally resell the tea to consuming country importers, packers, and the like. Other deals are struck on a large scale between governments, in counter-trade deals, and many other complex international trades and barters. Outside of China, better-quality teas tend to sell either at auction or in private-party deals. The chain of custody for these teas may be quite long, going from garden to trader to blender or packer, to wholesaler to retailer and, eventually, to the consumer.

In trade, as in virtually every other aspect of tea from cultivation to processing, the history and traditions of each origin country profoundly affect the manner and style in which business is conducted. This theme of individual character is consistent throughout the tea culture, and we believe it is one of the real beauties of tea.

CHAPTER 2

Tea Anecdotes and History

It is only fitting that such a complex beverage be surrounded by fanciful, original tales, that throughout the ages poetry should be written in its honor, and that its history be replete with stories of love, scandal, and warfare. For the tea lover, the history of tea is entertaining and insightful; for the tea purveyor it is a marketing dream come true.

Like the beverage itself, there is something in tea's history for every taste. And, like the flavor spectrum of tea, the ground covered in tea's history is so immense it cannot possibly be given fair due in these few pages. The following excerpts from the life of tea are only meant to whet your appetite.

The Eyelids of Bodhidharma and Other Tales of Tea's Beginnings

There are a wide variety of legends surrounding the discovery of tea as a beverage, but here are two of our favorites. The first, a Japanese legend, revolves around Bodhidharma, or Daruma, as he is sometimes called. Bodhidharma was akin to a Buddhist saint, and was responsible for bringing Buddhism from his native India to China, from which it eventually made its way to Japan. The legend has it that he had taken a vow to spend nine years staring at a wall in constant meditation. When only five years into his meditation, he experienced a moment of extreme tiredness (no kidding!). The monk's eyelids fluttered closed and he found himself dozing. When he awoke, he was quite angered at his weakness. In a fit of chagrin, he tore off his eyelids and cast them to the ground. (Pictures of Bodhidharma show a rather bug-eyed and ferocious-looking gentleman.) Where his eyelids landed a tea plant immediately sprouted. He then made an infused beverage from the leaves of this plant, and went on to successfully complete his meditation without another accidental nap. Regardless of whether one chooses to believe this myth or not, tea has long been an important part of Japanese Buddhism, and is certainly an aid in staying awake and alert during lengthy meditations.

The Chinese, on the other hand, have tea being

discovered by Shen Nung, a legendary emperor thought to have ruled about 2737 B.C. This industrious emperor is also credited with inventing the plow, refining agriculture and animal husbandry, developing herbal medicine, and a host of other ideas that lead to Chinese civilization. (Shen Nung is often referred to as the "Divine Husbandman.") This tea origin myth has the emperor boiling water to drink (his own peculiar habit, and a healthy one at that) when a tea leaf fell into his pot from a nearby plant, and infused in the water. The resulting drink was not only pleasant tasting but also stimulating, and soon became an important part of Shen Nung's herbal medicine.

At this point, it might be helpful to put wide-eyed monks and contemplative emperors aside, and address the botanical birthplace of tea. Tea is an indigenous plant throughout the forests of southeast Asia, where left to its own devices it becomes a tree up to 40-feet high. Tea's origins lie in an indefinite area to the southeast of the Tibetan plateau, and includes Szechuan, Yunnan, Burma, and Siam, and, of course, northeast India, where the Assam variety is found. From these original locations, tea has spread throughout the world and today is cultivated in areas as diverse as Washington state on the west coast of the United States and Guatemala in Central America.

The small-leafed China plant remains fairly truebred and has avoided much of the crossbreeding and hybridization that marks modern agriculture. The Assam variety, due to the colonization and farming efforts of the English in India has been the subject of much hybridization. (The English brought in numerous China variety plants, only to watch them fail miserably, before recognizing the equally fine qualities of the indigenous plant.) The most tampered-with tea plants are those found growing in the Shan States of Burma and Siam.

A Cupful of Tea History

By most reports, tea was first consumed as a beverage in China, sometime between 2700 B.C. and 220 A.D. (This remarkably broad estimate is in part attributable to the difficulty of pinning down historical references to tea, in the absence of a character in written Chinese specific to tea, until sometime in the T'ang dynasty.) In any event, by early in the 8th century, tea was clearly an important part of daily life in China, and was first taxed in 780 A.D. In the same year the first work specific to tea was published. The *Ch'a Ching* was written by Lu Yu, a poet and scholar commissioned by tea merchants to produce a volume encompassing the sum of contemporary tea knowledge. The work includes information about tea growing, processing, brewing, serving, and drinking.

Tea has remained a vital part of Chinese life and culture since this era. The style of cultivation, processing, and consumption has undergone numerous changes, each succeeding dynasty imparting some of the flavor of the contemporary period to all aspects of the product. The now traditional styles of green, black, and Oolong teas first made an appearance during the Ming dynasty.

Tea began to travel as a trade item as early as the fifth century, with some sources indicating Turkish traders bartering for tea on the Mongolian border. Certainly, tea was traded in this era within Mongolia and Tibet. Tea made its way to Japan late in the sixth century, along with another famous Chinese export, Buddhism. By the end of the seventh century, Buddhist monks were planting tea in Japan.

Tea first arrived in the west via overland trade into Russia, and to Holland via Japan. Certainly Arab traders had dealt in tea prior to this time, but no Europeans had a hand in tea as a trade item until the Dutch began an active and lucrative trade early in the 17th century. From Holland, tea spread relatively quickly throughout Europe. Oddly enough, although Russia had access to tea, it got off to a very slow start, and tea was already very popular in Europe before being embraced by Czarist Russia.

In the New World, tea made an early appearance in New Amsterdam, brought by the Dutch in the mid-17th century. Tea remained a very popular beverage throughout the newly colonized territories until the passage of the infamous 1765 Stamp Act and other taxation vehicles. Ultimately, the American resistance to tea taxes lead to the Boston Tea Party in 1773, and tea was forever associated with British imperialism in the minds of Americans.

From about 1650 onwards, the history of tea belongs in great part to the British. The Honourable East India Company, or the John Company as it came to be known, brought its first shipment of tea to England in about 1669, and, from a humble beginning of 140 pounds, tea quickly grew in popularity throughout the Empire until, by 1800, nearly 24 million pounds were being imported annually. This period saw tea at the center of both society and controversy, with great tea lovers like Dr. Samuel Johnson defending the attributes of tea from all attackers (and there were many). The British continued to occupy center stage in tea's history well into the twentieth century, and that great drama has featured everything from smuggling to opium wars to the remarkable story of the clipper ships.

Today, much to the surprise of most tea lovers, tea belongs to the Germans. Hamburg is a mecca for those pursuing fine teas. The large German trade houses have lately dominated the competition for acquiring the world's finest teas at auction and in private deals. The German people have embraced tea in much the same fashion Americans have embraced coffee beverages. Not only can you find the premier Spring Flush Darjeelings, Estate Ceylons, and world-class China teas, but Germany is also the thriving center of the flavored world.

Thomas Starts with Tea

We have a good friend who is a tea man from Taiwan. His family's legacy in the tea business goes back many generations. Like most modern Taiwanese he chose his own western name, opting for Thomas, because, as he points out, every modern tea man of significance seems to have been named Thomas. Here is a smattering of tea Thomases.

- Thomas Garway—the first English coffee house proprietor to offer tea.
- Thomas Rawlinson—Founder of Mitre Tavern, eventually to become Davison, Newman & Co.
- Thomas Twining—Proprietor of "Tom's," the first retail outlet for tea to welcome women.
- Thomas Lipton—The irascible Irishman who founded Lipton Teas.
- Thomas Sullivan—The serendipitous inventor of the tea bag.

The World of Tea

Tea is grown on a commercial basis in some forty countries around the world (see Fig. 3.1). Most of them have some history in the tea trade that accounts for their traditional types and styles of tea. What follows here is a brief look at some of the most important producing countries, and a look at some of the highlights of tea production by geography, style of manufacture, or other noteworthy points about one or more of the teas produced there. This is not meant (by any stretch of the imagination) to be a comprehensive guide. Enjoying tea is akin to enjoying traveling. You can read guidebooks and travel notes to get a general sense of your destination, but there is no substitute for the actual experience, and, finally, each person's perception of the experience is

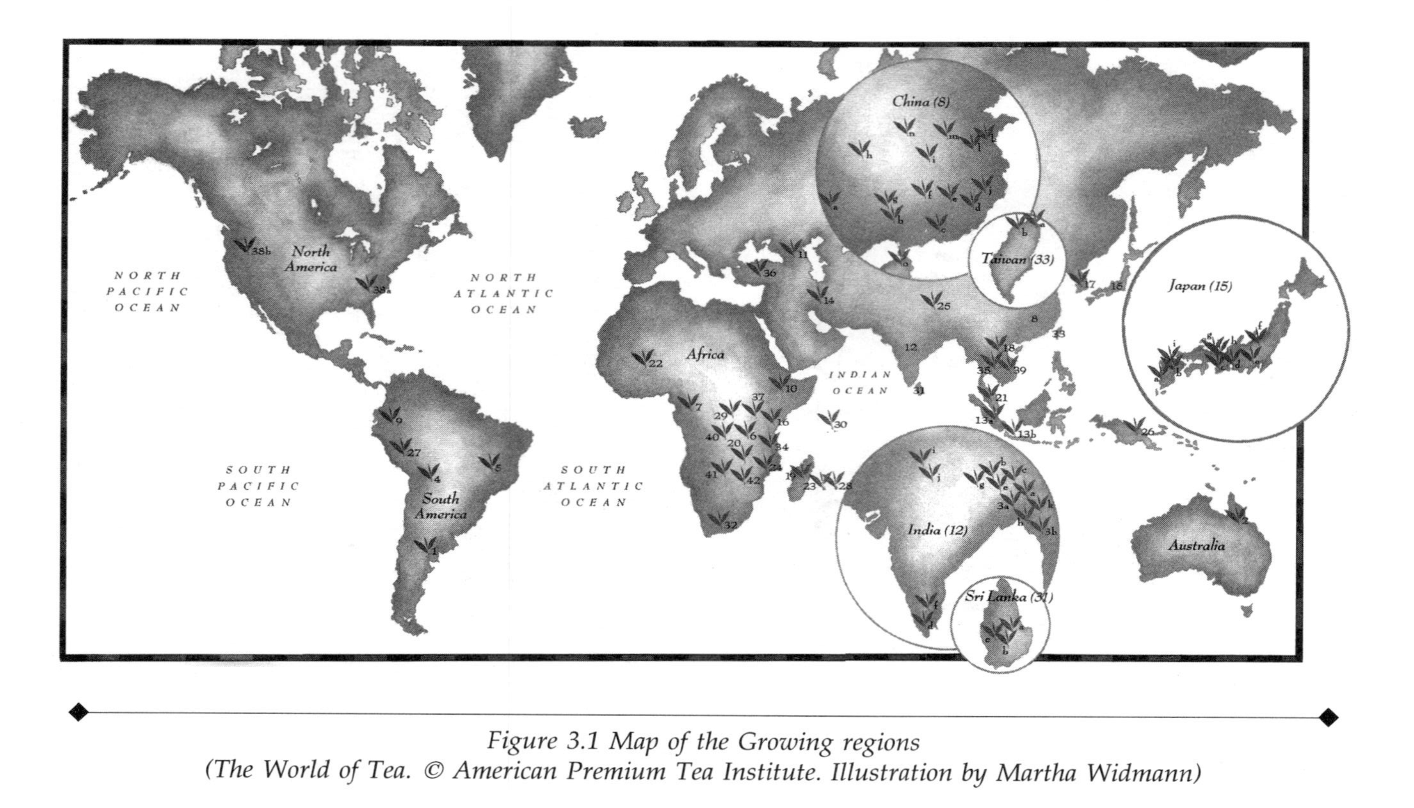

Figure 3.1 Map of the Growing regions
(The World of Tea. © American Premium Tea Institute. Illustration by Martha Widmann)

Legend—Tea Growing Countries

1. Argentina
2. Australia
   Queensland
3. Bangladesh
   a. Sylhet
   b. Chittagong
4. Bolivia
5. Brazil
6. Burundi
7. Cameroon
8. China
   a. Yunnan
   b. Guangxi
   c. Guangdong
   d. Fujian
   e. Jiangxi
   f. Hunan
   g. Guizhou
   h. Sichuan
   i. Hubei
   j. Zhejiang
   k. Jiangsu
   l. Anhui
   m. Henan
   n. Shaanxi
   o. Hainan
9. Ecuador
10. Ethiopia
11. Georgia/Russia
12. India
    a. Assam
    b. Darjeeling
    c. Sikkim
    d. Kerala
    e. Dooars
    f. Nilgiri
    g. Terai
    h. Cachar
    i. Kangra
    j. Dehra Dun
    k. Manispur
13. Indonesia
    a. Pematangsiantar
       Pengalengan Plateau
14. Iran
15. Japan
    a. Kagoshima
    b. Miyazaki
    c. Nara
    d. Miye
    e. Shizuoka
    f. Saitama
    g. Kyoto
    h. Yamashiro
    i. Fukuoka
16. Kenya
17. Korea (South)
18. Laos
19. Madagascar
20. Malawi
21. Malaysia
22. Mali (Republic of)
23. Mauritus
24. Mozambique
25. Nepal
26. Papua-New Guinea
27. Peru
28. Reunion
    (Indian Ocean)
29. Rwanda
30. Seychelles
    (Indian Ocean)
31. Sri Lanka
    a. Uva
    b. Dimbula
    c. Nuwara Eliya
32. South Africa
33. Taiwan
    a. T'ao-yuan
    b. Hsin-chu
34. Tanzania
35. Thailand
36. Turkey
37. Uganda
38. USA
    a. South Carolina
    b. Oregon
       (Experimental Station)
39. Vietnam
40. Zaire
41. Zambia
42. Zimbabwe

unique to them. Here, then, are some notable destinations in tea and some landmark teas that are produced there.

Tea-Producing Regions

India

India is the 800-pound gorilla of tea on both sides of the tea world, being both the largest producer and the largest consumer of tea overall (see Fig. 3.2). As might be expected, every possible range in quality and style is produced here, from CTC (crush, tear, and curl; see p. 15) to orthodox to green and even a smattering of Oolong teas. In 1995, India produced over 750,000 metric tons of tea, or about one-third of all the tea produced in the world. At the same time, domestic consumption in India continues to grow at a hectic pace. In 1995, India consumed 595,000 metric tons of its own product, and that number is estimated to be nearly 650,000 tons by the end of 1997. The production of tea in India is also increasing, with 1997 production estimated at a whopping 800,000 tons! Of all the tea produced in India, 99 percent is black tea, and of that nearly 90 percent is CTC.

As you can imagine, tea is of significant economic importance to India. Tea not only accounts for 1 percent of all Indian exports but also is the largest employer in the organized agriculture sector. Some 1.2 million people have direct, permanent employment on tea estates, and a total of almost 6 million reside on estate lands. Land dedicated to tea production has a gross total of almost 2 million acres, with well over 1 million acres under cultivation. There are some 35,000 tea estates active in producing tea in India, the vast majority of which are small family holdings of less than 125 acres. New estates are being planted,

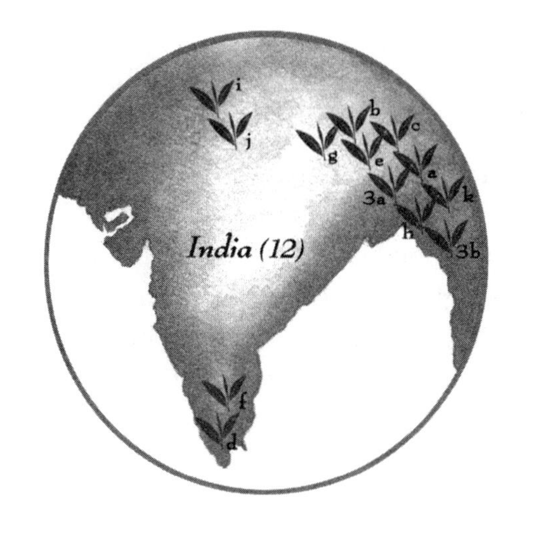

Figure 3.2 Map of India (Illustration by Martha Widmann)

primarily in northern India in the Dooars and Terai belt of West Bengal, in an effort to keep pace with growing consumption.

India is a large country of very diverse geography and climate, and its teas reflect this. They range from rather plain, uninteresting teas grown for commercial use and processed as CTC teas, to some of the most extraordinary fine leaf teas anywhere in the world. The tiny Darjeeling area in northern India produces little more than 10,000 tons of tea annually, but it is so prized amongst the tea community, and has such an enormous reputation, that, by most reckoning, five times that amount is sold as "Darjeeling" annually. If imitation is the sincerest form of flattery, than Darjeeling teas are the most flattered teas in the world.

ASSAM

Teas from India are generally divided into two broad regional types, north Indian and south Indian teas. The north Indian teas include most of the famous and recognized growing regions. The largest of these, the *Assam* Valley, includes seven or more distinct regions which are often lumped together and referred to as Assam teas.

Taster's Notes: The orthodox teas of Assam are generally well made, grayish to black in color, and often have gold colored tip apparent in the better grades. Assam teas produce strong, intense cups of malty, bright, and rich tea, with the very best yielding rich, thick cups with a wide range of flavor and aroma notes. Some carry a rich, honeyed flavor, and can be excellent self-drinkers; that is, they make a great cup of tea by themselves. The teas of Assam are very useful for blending, providing a solid foundation on which to build a blend, and are traditionally the base for Irish Breakfast blends. In recent years, they have become more widely available as origin teas and can be found sold by estate name and even by which flush they were produced from.

DARJEELING

The famous *Darjeeling* district is nestled in the foothills of the Himalayas, northwest of Assam. Here some 78 gardens produce distinctive black teas of exclusively orthodox manufacture. It is here in Darjeeling, perhaps more than any other place in the world, that the tea maker's art can best be compared with that of the wine maker. The fine hand of the garden manager can be detected in the produce of many gardens, and, occasionally, when a manager changes properties, he seems to take his unique style and flavors with him.

Taster's Notes: Generally, Darjeeling teas are intensely aromatic, flavorful teas with a characteristic muscat flavor note. There are pointed differences in cup characteristics between the first flush teas, plucked from March through April, and ensuing flushes. First flush or Spring Flush teas are marked by an intensely aromatic cup, with an overall pleasantly astringent mouth feel, and a relatively lightly colored cup. These teas cast an amber liquor, ranging from a pale yellowish orange to a deeper amber hue. The taste of a new round of growth after the winter dormancy is readily apparent in the best of the first flush teas. The second flush, or *Summer Flush* tea, is generally plucked from May through early July, and tends to be equally as complex, if somewhat more rounded than the first flush, and is accompanied by a much heavier weight. The best teas from a good year result in a cup which is unparalleled in the tea world. Prices generally reflect this.

Life on a Darjeeling Garden

It is sometimes difficult for us to truly appreciate the scale of human effort that goes into creating great tea. An incredible number of people are involved in the cultivation, harvesting, and processing of tea, and, in the case of the Darjeeling region, tea is a way of life.

The famous tea plantations, or gardens, of northern India are, in effect, small nearly self-contained cities. The typical garden is home to a community of workers and their families, numbering in the thousands. Darjeeling is a relatively remote area situated in the rugged terrain of the Himalayan foothills, and travel is difficult; thus each garden must provide for the basic necessities of daily life.

Garden workers live in well-kept, modest homes and enjoy a reasonable standard of living, particularly when compared with the extreme poverty of much of the Indian subcontinent. The most progressive gardens offer such benefits as paid maternity leave, nursery facilities, and medical care. All gardens provide access to government schools, and child labor is prohibited.

The responsibility for the economic health of these small cities rests on the shoulders of the planter. By necessity, he is a renaissance man, part agriculturist, part engineer, and a skilled administrator. Ultimately, he is responsible not only for the general agricultural practices of the garden but also for the manufacturing facilities, the management of an enormous labor force, the construction of roads on the estate, and quite often the construction of buildings.

OTHER INDIAN TEAS

Northwest of the Assam Valley lies the *Sikkim* growing area, where teas similar in character and leaf style to Darjeeling are produced. One Sikkim garden, Temi, is well known for it's export quality teas.

> **Taster's Notes:** *Temi* tea is like a muted Darjeeling in flavor, with a somewhat heavier body. It has a very Darjeeling-like appearance, which makes perfect sense, as it is essentially across the street from the eastern border of the Darjeeling district.

South of Darjeeling lies *Dooars*, the second largest growing region in India. The majority of tea produced in this low lying region is processed into CTC teas destined primarily for tea bags.

> **Taster's Notes:** The few orthodox teas made here are similar in style to the teas of Assam, very dark and full bodied, although generally not reaching the quality of better Assam teas.

Terai occupies a flat plain south of Darjeeling, and produces nearly 30,000 metric tons of black tea.

> **Taster's Notes:** Terai tea at its best is dark, rich, and spicy, producing a thick liquor that stands up well to milk.

Far to the south, in the very southern tip of the Indian peninsula, lies the *Nilgiri* region. Nilgiri teas are a relative unknown in the premium tea community, but they are generally very useful blenders, making their presence felt throughout any blend that contains them. They are seldom seen as self-drinking teas here in the U.S., appearing primarily as blends.

> **Taster's Notes:** The orthodox teas from this region (Blue Mountains in Tamil) are bright and colory, with good flavor. While they are distinctively different from Ceylons, they share many of their more positive qualities. We have enjoyed a number of them, and find their bright, light cups easy to drink and pleasant.

There are several other distinct tea-producing regions scattered around the massive Indian land mass, but most of them produce teas destined for blending and tea bags.

Ceylon

The island nation of Sri Lanka, or *Ceylon* as it is still referred to in the tea trade, is the third largest producer of teas in the world, with an annual production nearing 300,000 metric tons, and the largest exporter (see Fig. 3.3). Nearly all of this is black tea, ranging in quality from superb to quite plain. Ceylon is the youngest of the old tea-growing countries. Up until 1869, Ceylon was a thriving coffee producer, but disease destroyed the coffee plantations, and tea was in-

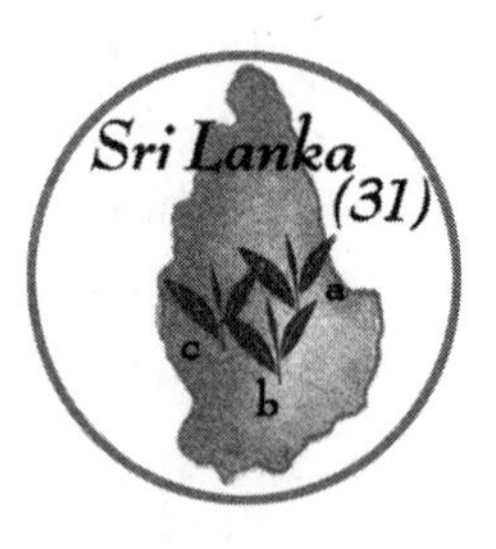

Figure 3.3 Map of Ceylon (Illustration by Martha Widmann)

troduced to replace it. The lion's share of tea produced there is CTC, but many fine orthodox teas are still manufactured. They can be broadly classified by altitude (high, low, or medium grown), or by geography (Uva, Dimbula, Nuwara, Eliya). In the case of the high-grown teas in particular, there is a profound seasonality which influences quality. An even more profound impact on quality was a government scheme to nationalize the tea estates. In recent years, the majority have gone back to private hands, and much of the quality has returned to the tea.

Ceylon came into its own as a major producer in large part due to the efforts of one Sir Thomas Lipton. Lipton saw the potential for tea in Ceylon, and bought a number of tea estates there. What he didn't buy outright, he bought from, and brought twenty-thousand chests of Ceylon tea to England in 1891. His enthusiastic and seemingly endless marketing of Ceylon teas not only successfully introduced them to the market but also made them forever associated with a leaf size grading designation, Orange Pekoe, known in the trade as OP and having nothing to do with orange in terms of color or flavor. He also seized upon their hallmark cup characteristic, brightness, and sold them as "brisk" teas for well under the current market.

Ceylon teas are, in general, well-twisted, wiry, long leaves that are very easily identified by sight. The broken grades are extremely popular as blenders, adding flavor, color, and brightness to almost any blend. About 40 percent of the estates are located at altitudes above 4000 feet, and their high-grown nature comes through in the cup as an intense brightness.

Many of the better gardens are marketed by name in the United States, so look for familiar favorites like Kenilworth, Pettiagalla, and Berubeula. As in all teas, leaf grade is not always a reliable indicator of quality, and many BOP Ceylon's cup well. (See pages 62–66 for more information on all of the various leaf grades.)

Taster's Notes: Ceylon continues to produce teas much like those that Lipton marketed. Their most universal quality is that they tend to be very bright and flavory, and throw very colory cups. There are precious few self-drinkers amongst them, but those that exist are wonderfully accessible and utilitarian. Our favorite, the OP from *Kenilworth,* is a mainstay of our tea cabinet, and is consumed straight or blended nearly every day. It is a bright, lively tea, well made, although not high grown. In the cup, it is unusually well balanced for a

Ceylon, which frequently lacks weight and complexity.

China

China is the birthplace of tea, and nowhere else in the world is there so much diversity in style and grade as can be found here (see Fig. 3.4). The Chinese expression for *a great many* is "ten thousand," and both are probably correct answers to the question "How many different teas are made in China?" Tea is produced in at least 15 of China's provinces, and all of them have one or more truly notable teas. About two-thirds of the 650,000 metric tons produced annually is green tea, with the balance about evenly divided

Figure 3.4 Map of China (Illustration by Martha Widmann)

between blacks and oolongs. Green teas are by far the choice for domestic consumption, followed by oolong. Most of the black-tea production is exported. To truly do justice to all the great teas produced in China would require a whole separate book, but we have listed here some of our personal favorites, as well as some that just need mentioning.

ANHUI

Anhui province produces a tremendous amount of tea in a wide variety of styles, but its most famous tea is undoubtedly *Keemun*. These distinctive, well-made black teas range in quality from fair to exquisite. The lower grades are good blenders, and make frequent appearances as a base for iced tea in the United States.

> **Taster's Notes:** The top grades, lead by the Hao Ya series, are hugely aromatic, distinctive teas, easily identified by their subtle smoky aroma and intense flavor. The leaf style ranges from fair to extremely well made, with the top grades making a beautiful presentation, featuring tiny, twisted leaves of very consistent manufacture.

FUJIAN

The *Fujian* province produces such a wide array of unique and special teas that they are generally divided by Northern Fujian (Min Bei) and Southern Fujian (Min Nam) types.

Taster's Notes: Both north and south are reasonably famous for their *Jasmine* teas, and Fujian is noted as being the birthplace of Jasmine teas. The best of them are generally made from *Pouchong*-style leaf (a very lightly oxidized oolong style), and are repeatedly scented with jasmine flowers. In the top grades, the flowers are introduced to the tea and then removed after imparting their fragrance to the leaves, a process that may be repeated as many as seven times. In fact, a handy rule of thumb when buying good Jasmine teas is that the less flowers present, the better the quality. The top grades of Fujian Jasmines are exquisite, delicate teas which produce a pale cup redolent with the fresh scent of jasmine.

Ti Kuan Yin, the Iron Goddess of Mercy, is widely produced in Northern Fujian. This oolong tea tends to be of a very different character from those produced in Taiwan, somewhat less delicate and sweet, but still pure and clean in character. The dark, tightly twisted leaves yield a light red cup that is slightly astringent, but well-rounded, sweet, and accessible. The name Ti Kuan Yin, taken from a legend involving a Buddhist goddess, is often applied to the strain of bush it is produced from.

Lapsang Souchong, a distinctively smoky, tarry-flavored, black tea is another famous product of the Fujian province. The tea derives its smoky flavor from being processed over pine root fires, and the large leaf presents a red cup with deep, rich tones somewhat more reminiscent of coffee than of tea.

Other Chinese Teas

Yunnan produces a variety of black teas, a few of which find their way into the United States as leaf teas. They are also excellent contributors to blends, although not in a traditional China black fashion. Yunnan is famous for its ancient tea trees, some of which have grown to incredible heights (by tea-bush standards). The particular strain of tea commonly grown there is also used for another famous tea, *Pu-erh*. Pu-erh is one of the more ancient tea styles in China. It is manufactured exclusively from the broad-leafed strain of tea indigenous to Yunnan, and has been attributed many medicinal properties in Chinese herbal lore. It is gaining steadily in popularity in the United States, and many different variations are available.

Pu-erh is often pressed into bricks or into *tou-cha*, or bowl-shaped cakes. It has a very distinctive, earthy, even musty flavor, and is highly prized by the Chinese. Flavor ranges from intensely earthy to somewhat lighter in character, and it can be a difficult tea for western palates to appreciate.

Taster's Notes: Teas from Yunnan have an interesting, peppery flavor note, and the best of them are good self-drinkers.

Green teas account for the vast majority of Chinese teas, and they take a seemingly endless variety of shapes, styles and flavors. Some that are frequently found in the United States and are of special note, are *Lung Ching* (Dragon Well) from the West Lake district of Zhejiang province, *Pi Lo Chun* (Green Snail Spring) from the mountainous area near Lake Taihu, also in Zhejiang, and *Gunpowder,* from Zhejiang province, south of Shanghai. Gunpowder teas range from tiny pinhead styles, to large, lower grade Imperials. The best of the lot, *Temple of Heaven,* is widely available in the United States.

We must note again that these brief descriptions and short list of teas cannot begin to do justice to the incredible diversity of China teas. Only a lifetime of study could begin to unravel all that these teas have to offer, but, with ever increasing availability here in the United States, they are a fascinating reflection, not only of Chinese culture, but also of the long history of tea in China.

Japan

Japan first saw tea along with another famous Chinese export, Buddhism. Buddhist monks brought tea, tea culture, and ultimately tea plants to Japan late in the sixth century, and after a period of disfavor, it was embraced by the Japanese strongly in the twelfth century. Ceremonial tastings, contests, and finally the highly developed *Cha-no-yu,* or Japanese tea ceremony, arose from Japan's love affair with all things tea (see Fig. 3.5).

Virtually all the tea made in Japan is green tea. It is rigidly graded into *Gyokuro, Sencha,* and *Bancha* grades. *Gyokuro,* or Pearl Dew, is the most prized and is grown under shade in the Uji district of Honshu. The tea is steam fired to denature it, and then basket fired by hand and rolled. Because of the intense hand labor involved, and high demand in Japan, Gyokuro is very expensive. Sencha teas are made in much the same fashion, without shading, and with significantly less hand labor, and they are generally pan fired. Sencha is produced only from first and second flush pluckings. Bancha teas are the everyday teas of Japan, made from later pluckings and somewhat coarser in

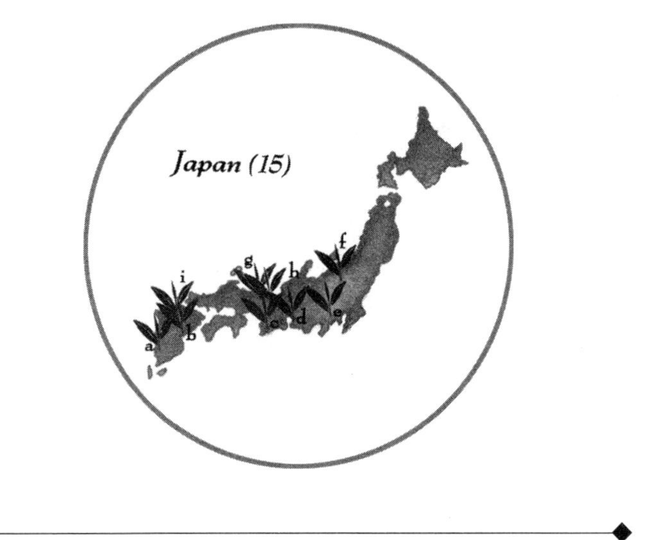

Figure 3.5 Map of Japan (Illustration by Martha Widmann)

flavor and appearance. The final round of mechanized plucking, or shearing, is used to make *Koki cha,* or twig tea.

Besides these graded teas, others are made in a variety of fashions. Powdered Gyokuro is made for the Japanese tea ceremony, and is called *Matcha.* It is not technically exported from Japan, but if you ever have the chance to attend the traditional Japanese tea ceremony, it will be properly served there. It is frothed into cool (by tea standards) water, and yields a thick, foamy beverage that is interesting but not typical of great green tea. *Genmaicha* is made by blending medium quality Sencha with toasted rice, which produces a very palatable tea based beverage. *Hojicha* is made by roasting finished tea leaves, imparting a brown color to the leaves, which yield a light, smooth liquor.

Japan produces about 98,000 metric tons of tea annually, which meets about two-thirds of the domestic demand. Another 50,000 or so tons is imported annually, primarily from Taiwan, China, and Brazil.

Taster's Notes: The cup from Gyokuro is pale green to yellow, the flavor is astringent and vegetal. Brewed properly, with somewhat cooler water, there are faint sweet notes, but in general it is incredibly crisp and clean, with a distinctive grassy flavor and aroma.

Sencha tea generally yields clear, pale-green cups that carry many of the same vegetal, grassy notes common to all Japanese teas. This can be a somewhat difficult flavor for westerners to appreciate, but, over time, we have come to enjoy it tremendously.

Taiwan

The island nation of Taiwan, still known as *Formosa* to much of the rather hidebound tea trade, lies off the east coast of China, about 750 miles southwest of Japan (see Fig. 3.6). The island encompasses about 13,500 square miles of territory, and is roughly bisected by a central mountain range. The population of 21 million is made up primarily of Chinese settlers from the Fujian province, an area with its own tea treasures, as well as Cantonese, and, starting in 1949, many military and government staff who followed Chiang Kai-shek from the mainland. There are also approximately 1.5 million aboriginal peoples still living in Taiwan.

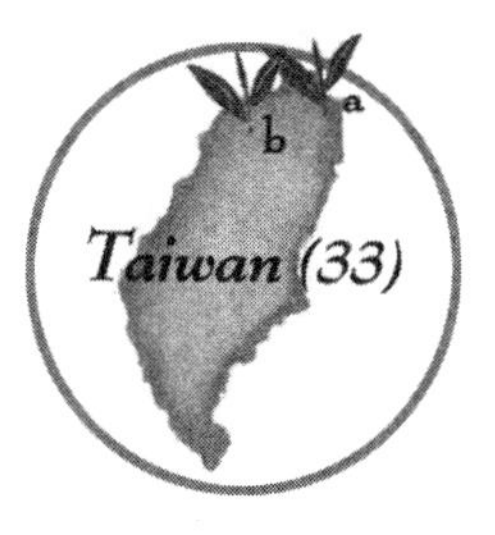

Figure 3.6 Map of Taiwan (Illustration by Martha Widmann)

There are some 21,000 acres under tea cultivation in Taiwan, and they produce about 20,000 metric tons of tea annually. The vast majority (about 91 percent) and the best of this is oolong tea; this production is regarded as the finest oolong tea in the world. Another 8 percent of production is in green tea, in many of the traditional Chinese styles, including Gunpowder, Chun Mee, Pi Lo Chun, Dragon Well, pan-fired types, as well as Sencha and Bancha, steam-fired types for Japanese export. The remaining 1 percent is black tea production, of a type that is relatively unknown to tea consumers. Some broken pekoe black tea from Taiwan finds its way into some very famous flavored tea blends.

Taiwan has a large appetite for its own tea, consuming about 98 percent of the production domestically. Moreover, unlike many producing countries, domestic tastes run strongly in favor of higher-quality teas, and there is very little production dedicated to broken-leaf types destined for mass market tea bag use. Exports of Taiwan tea were very important economically from 1945 until 1968, serving as the largest foreign currency industry on the island, but, since then, an increasing middle class and burgeoning trade in the high-tech sector have greatly reduced tea's importance as an export item. Taiwan tea producers are a tough lot, as the domestic market is less lucrative and much more highly competitive than in the past.

When tea people talk about Taiwan, they are almost always talking about oolong teas. Formosa oolong teas of the fancy grades are not only generally regarded as the best oolongs in the world, but they are often considered to be amongst the very best teas of any style. Oolong production involves highly specialized skills in the control of the withering, oxidizing, and firing. In Taiwan oolongs, oxidation covers a broad range, from 15 to 70 percent, giving each variety a distinctive aroma, flavor, color and finish.

In Taiwan, amber and jade oolong teas are traditionally enjoyed in the *gongfu style,* most often in Yixing pots, in which the leaves are infused very briefly with hot water, which is then poured off. The leaves are then reinfused, and the tea is poured after about a minute. The leaves may be reinfused several times, with each resulting infusion yielding a very different liquor from the first. When enjoying Taiwan teas as tea drinkers, we often prepare them in this fashion. However, when tasting the tea for evaluation, we use the standard cupping methodology outlined in Chapter 5. White Tip oolongs, which did not gain tremendous domestic popularity until recent years, are more commonly prepared in western fashion using porcelain tea sets.

It is worth noting that, in Taiwan, the making of oolong teas is regarded as a precious art, one that requires years of expert training. From the nursing of a seedling, to planting, to nourishing the bushes, to properly selecting the best time to pluck the leaves, the husbandry of the tea farmer is a legacy passed down from many generations. Only the application of years of dedicated study and practice, combined with the unique nature of the Formosa tea leaves, can produce the exceptional-quality oolong teas that have made the island's teas famous.

When buying Taiwan oolong teas, look for large, lightly to well-rolled leaves, with the presence of silver tips being a plus, and the presence of a lot of stem being a negative. The dry leaf should give a good indication of the degree of oxidation, and many very fancy styles will be labeled to reflect this on a percentage basis. The aroma of the dry leaf will also give an indication of the resulting liquor. More heavily fired types have a distinctive bakey note, and tend to produce heavy, less sweet cups. The more highly oxidized types have a distinctive light fruit aroma, and often produce fragrant, sweet cups with nuances of peach and almond. The best greenish styles have a spicy aroma, and can yield cups of incredible delicacy and nuance, with all the lively top notes of a green tea backed up by the sweet, subtle fragrance of oolong.

Grading Formosa Oolong

The teas of Taiwan, in particular the great oolongs, are at once the most clearly defined and most nebulous of teas. The nomenclature associated with the teas ranges from very direct to downright confusing. The grades established by various government agencies have rarely coincided with the grades recognized or accepted by the trade. The efforts of the Taiwan tea trade have resulted in some additional confusion, although their intent is certainly to clarify the stylistic differences within the oolong category. On the other hand, one taste of a great oolong next to a poorer quality type is enough to reveal the massive differences in flavor, aroma, and general appeal.

In his classic 1935 work, *All About Tea*, William Ukers gives the following grading designations for Formosa oolongs:

> *From the Formosan Government Tea Inspection Office—Standard, On Good, Good, Fully Good, Good Up, Good to Superior, On Superior, Superior, Fully Superior, Superior Up, Superior to Fine, Fine, Fine Up, Fine to Finest, Finest, Finest to Choice, Choice. The trade also recognizes several intermediary gradings, such as Good Leaf, Fully Standard, Standard to Good, Strictly Superior, Choicest, and Fancy.*

Today the grade names generally encountered in the industry range upward in quality, starting from Standard and followed by Choice, Choicest, Fancy, and Fanciest. At the consumer level, many Formosa oolong teas are sold by other names, sometimes indicating their quality or style, sometimes their regional origin, or, most frequently, the marketing efforts of the vendor. Still, there is no need for despair, as top-quality oolong teas are easily recognizable for their exquisite taste. Just ask for a sample, and make your own determination.

Taster's Notes: *Jade Oolong* is very slightly oxidized, with an elegant natural aroma and fresh flavor. *Pouchong* types are partially rolled, while *Tung Ting* types are well rolled. Unique pan firing produces a bright golden colored cup which is smooth, with a sweet, lingering finish. *Amber Oolong* is the product of medium oxidation combined with a careful charcoal firing to produce an amber colored cup that has fruity aroma and a toasty flavor.

White Tip Oolong, sometimes called "the champagne of teas," is unique and rare, harvested only within the first 15 days of July each year, with only a fine plucking of two leaves and the white tipped buds. These are oxidized to about 70 percent, and yield a bright gold to orange cup with a smooth, deliciously fruity flavor, and a floral aroma laced with sweetness of ripe peaches.

Other Countries of Interest

The five producing countries detailed above account for nearly two-thirds of all the world's teas and, as far as we know 100 percent of the premium or specialty teas. However tea is produced in some 35 other countries, and we should mention some of them here. Kenya has become one of the largest exporters of tea today, producing 285,000 metric tons of tea annually and exporting nearly all of it. Very nearly all of the tea produced there is CTC. Kenya teas are very bright and distinctively flavored, and are in high demand as blenders for tea bag packing. Other African countries, like Malawi, have enjoyed similar, if not as dramatic success in growing tea.

Indonesia has a long history in the tea trade and today produces about 160,000 tons of tea, ranging in quality from poor to excellent. About 33,000 tons of this is green tea, some of which is exported to Japan.

Turkey produces 126,000 tons of tea but consumes about 90 percent of its production internally. The tea manufactured there are of generally poor quality and often face an ignominious ending, boiled into a tragically thick and bitter liquor, then sweetened prior to consumption.

Argentina makes it onto the tea map through the dubious distinction of being the largest exporter of tea to the U.S. market. Most of the poor quality, albeit innocuous, teas produced there end up in commercial tea bags, as RTD (ready to drink), or as bottled iced-tea beverages.

CHAPTER 4

Finding the Truly Exceptional Cup

Americans are not big consumers of tea, and most of what they do consume is in the form of ready-to-drink (RTD) iced tea. What little hot tea they drink is almost all in the form of tea bags. We believe that tea bags are a wonderful little invention, and incredibly convenient. In fact, in the current tea environment in the United States, you are probably as likely to get a good cup of tea out of a tea bag as you are out of loose tea. This is primarily due to the scarcity of good loose leaf tea here, combined with storage and handling issues.

It doesn't have to be this way. There are now more vendors of loose leaf tea actively promoting their products than there have been since before WWII. Many of them have a wide selection of exciting teas from all over the globe, and some lists are so long and extensive as to be nearly impossible to decipher. With a little background information on how tea is named, graded, and properly prepared and stored, you can enjoy myriad fine teas with very little confusion or risk. Well, not too much confusion. Read on.

Tea Grading: What's in a Name?

BOP, FOP, TGFOP, GBOP, OP, and so on, and so on. No, these are not typographical errors or the mindless pecking of monkeys at the keyboard trying to emulate Shakespeare. These are actually grading designations for black teas. How to decipher them, and what information they really provide, is what we will attempt to explain here.

As a first step, we should consider some other grading systems for foods and beverages. Wine, for example, is graded differently depending on the whims of the producing country. In France, the *appellation controllee* system is used to communicate the provenance of a particular wine. Essentially, this system will describe where the wine grapes were grown, who processed them into wine, and who bottled or blended them. Closer inspection of the details of this system will reveal some rough idea of the varieties of grapes used, the generally accepted rating of the producers, and a muddled outlook on the likely overall quality of the wine in question. By contrast, in Germany, there is a very tightly controlled and clearly articulated quality rating system that will allow even a layman to inspect a wine label and gain a good indication of the quality of the bottle in hand. Most other wine-producing countries have some often-disputed, generally highly politicized, and seldom very useful system of grading, labeling, or classification.

Coffee is also graded in various forms in most of the countries in which it is produced. In a few enlightened regions, green (unroasted) coffee may carry a grade that designates the altitude range at which it was grown and, sometimes, the particular region from which it came. Most generally, however, coffee is graded by bean size. While this is a rough indicator of the relative health of the parent tree, it is by no means a clear indicator of quality. The infamous Colombian Supremo is, in fact, a size designation, and the resultant quality of the coffee varies widely from region to region, as well as from one harvest to the next.

Tea shares the misfortune of these other products, inasmuch as such grading systems that do exist focus generally on the size and style of the processed leaf. This is at best an indicator of *potential* quality and, at worst, a marketing gimmick used to sell poor quality teas at inflated prices. Even so, it serves the quality-conscious tea consumer to be able to decipher the letters which may precede the name of teas they are being offered. Here, then, is a breakdown of the letter designations and what they are supposed to mean.

Tea Grades

D is for *dust*. This is just what it sounds like—the tiny particles of broken tea leaves. Processed tea becomes increasingly brittle as moisture is lost in the process, and one of the results is a collection of these tiny pieces. Dust has value as an ingredient in tea bags, because the very small particles have enormous surface area relative to their weight. This means they infuse very rapidly and yield a strong, darkly colored liquor. Unfortunately, the same mathematics of surface area and rapid infusion mean that the less pleasant flavors present in tea also appear in the cup.

FNGS is for *fannings*. These are incrementally larger pieces of dust, which share the same performance qualities in tea bags, and yield similarly poor cups of tea.

BOP is for *broken orange pekoe,* pronounced "peck-o." These are considerably larger pieces of the broken leaves, and can be very good if the original leaf was of high quality. These broken pieces are slower to infuse than dust or fannings but faster than larger grades. Many fine teas are available as BOP and they can be exceptional.

OP is for strictly *orange pekoe*. These are whole-leaf teas, which may or may not result from the plucking of the second leaf, as opposed to the strict two leaves and a bud qualifier. Much slower to infuse than the broken grades, they may be excellent, provided that the other quality factors are present. In short, a tea that tastes good as a BOP will be even better in its OP form.

FOP is for *flowery orange pekoe*. This term indicates the presence of the flower leaf, or first open leaf. This is generally a positive attribute, although, once again, other quality factors must be present.

G is for *golden*. This term may appear before one of the broken or leaf grades and refers to the presence of yellowish pieces of the leaf bud in sufficient quantity to be easily seen by the naked eye. Thus, a GBOP is a *golden broken orange pekoe* tea, comprised of relatively large broken pieces of the whole leaves and substantial amount of the golden tips of the leaf bud. This is a good indicator of quality, but hardly a guarantee.

T is for *tippy*. This indicates a substantial presence of the whole leaf bud, which may be greenish, black, silver, or golden depending on the origin of the tea, processing methodology, relative maturity of the leaf bud, and a few other factors. Many fine teas are presented as TGFOP, which, from our perspective, is the highest grade to have any objective reality. Other letters may precede these but they are generally the result of some marketer's high flown flights of fancy.

Now, for the bad news . . . after digesting this alphabet soup, be prepared to disregard all of it with any oolong or green tea, and many black teas from certain origins. This is just as well, because, ultimately, the quality of any tea can only be judged in the cup.

How to Taste Tea Like the Pros

The *cupping* of tea, as professionals refer to their ritualistic slurping, is one of the most important tools used to establish the character and relative value of tea. In the United States, for example, strict quality-control measures used to require that each tea be sampled or cupped prior to entry into the country. This was meant not only to insure the American consumer of a certain grade of tea, regrettably not always the best, but also to protect the tea from tampering. Like all businesses, tea has its handful of rotten people who, in the interest of gaining a few more pennies, might add vegetation or even recycled tea leaves to their product. Luckily, we don't know any of them.

However, purity of product is not the primary reason for learning how to evaluate teas in a professional manner. Consumers are in a better position to evaluate the tea they drink, and contrast and compare offerings of similar products if they are familiar with cupping procedures. So, let's begin. . . .

Cupping tea requires a few basic tools: a kettle, a measuring teaspoon or scale, cups and spoons. The cups should be simple, preferably without a handle, so that you can tell by touch when the liquid is cool enough to taste, and to prevent any shadows from being cast into the cup. The cups should also be white to achieve the truest possible color. Finally, you should have access to a sink or spittoon, so that you can spit the tea out easily and quickly after tasting it.

Most nonprofessionals may think that cupping tea requires swallowing the liquid, and therefore floating away or disappearing in a puff of caffeine-laden smoke. All taste sensations are registered on the tongue and through your sense of smell, so swallowing is not only unnecessary but also, when you are tasting a number of teas, may actually become unpleasant. If you are reserved about the idea of spitting, this exercise might best be practiced in private or you may want to prepare for some rather lively, caffeine-intoxicated afternoons; for those of you readers who are not so shy, spit away.

Budding afficionados should begin by sampling

Figure 4.1 A traditional tea tasting, or liquoring, being set up by an assistant in a tea garden cupping room (© Ambootia, Photographer: James Prinz, Chicago)

six teas per cupping session; any more can become confusing. It is also wise to compare teas that are fairly similar. It makes little sense to compare greens, oolongs, and blacks. We also suggest cupping with a friend, to benefit from a second opinion. Warning: Tasting tea with more than two people can make the undertaking more of a chore than a pleasure, as attested to by the old tea cliché: Too many tasters spoil the cup.

So, you've gotten your equipment, your teas, and a friend—from here cupping tea is pretty straightforward. The key is being well-organized. First, line up six six-ounce cups next to the sink, making sure they are well-rinsed (soapy residue can affect the taste of tea). Line up the samples to be tasted behind each cup. Make a card for each sample, to keep counter-space clear (see Fig. 4.1).

Before going any further, it's worth noting that in addition to the tasting of tea, there is also an entire arena of tea testing known as *dry-leaf analysis*. For our purposes, suffice it to say that the freshness of a tea can be determined by gently squeezing the leaves in the palm of your hand. Fresher teas will spring back quickly, whereas older tea leaves will crumble. You may also want to gently exhale upon them, letting the warmth of your breath bring some of the aromatics to life.

Now, measure a level teaspoon of each sample tea into the bottom of each cup. To be more precise, the sample should be weighed rather than measured, since the leaves may vary in volume and render the measurements unequal. If you use a scale, each cup should receive between two and three grams, roughly the weight of a dime.

Tasting will require a little more than a quart of water. Since water makes up 99 percent of the beverage, it is crucial to use water free of any flavor or odor taints. This simple standard unfortunately removes most of the tap water in the United States from the list of acceptable sources. If you plan to taste or cup tea regularly, or if you want to be a purist about the pursuit of drinking fine teas, you should consider investing in a good bottled-water service or a reverse-osmosis filter system. (Note that too much filtering of the water will cause tea to brew flat.) If you do use tap water, be sure that it is aerated—allow it to run for a couple of minutes, so that it is cold and clear of any water left standing in the pipes. (See Chapter 6 for a more thorough discussion of water.)

Bring the water to a full boil, then pour it over the leaves. This rule doesn't apply to tasting green teas; in this case you should let the kettle sit for a few minutes before pouring. This slightly cooler temperature will produce less harsh and, therefore, better-tasting green teas. For proper comparison, each cup of tea should be brewed with water of the same temperature. But then, in the ideal world, tap water would be suitable, wouldn't it?

After pouring the boiling water, let the tea steep for a fixed time—generally five minutes. Watching the tea leaves unfurl in the hot water is referred to poetically as watching "the agony of the leaves." This can tell the professional taster much about the processing and quality of the tea leaf. For the tea lover, it is simply a fascinating prelude to the enjoyment of freshly infused tea. After you have witnessed this graceful unfurling, lift the wet or, *infused,* leaves up from the bottom of the cup. Examine the leaves both visually and aromatically, and record your impressions as precisely as possible. The color should be bright and even—dull, uneven, or mixed color indicates a poor brew. The aroma will vary greatly, from "biscuity" to "black currant," depending on the tea being sampled. Repeat this for each tea you are tasting, dipping your spoon in a cup of clean water in between sampling.

You are now ready to taste the actual *liquor*. Bring a tablespoon of liquid to your mouth and slurp it with a loud noise. This rudeness is more important than you might think, because it ensures that you have created enough force to spray the tea over your entire tongue and into the back of your mouth. Different parts of the tongue will bring you different taste sensations. The back of the tongue senses bitterness, while the tip senses specific flavor characteristics. Spraying the back of your mouth allows the aromatic sensations of the tea to be reexperienced through your nasal passages. Having joyfully slurped the tea, swish it around in your mouth. This exercise will give you a sense of the tea's astringency. Finally, spit out the tea.

We personally find that taking a second slurp will leave you with a stronger impression, and it will often take more than one taste simply to clear your palate of the previous sample. However, keep in mind that like any muscle or sensory organ, you can tire out your taste buds and olfactory senses, so keep your impressions limited to a couple of tries per tea.

Like coffee and wine tasting, tea tasting has a language all its own. Before you can successfully evaluate tea through cupping you will have to have a tea vocabulary. Although it is easy to fall into generalizing tastings as "mmmmm" and "yuk," these won't help you remember your experiences in the future. For this reason, we have included a short glossary of tea-tasting terms in Appendix A. These cover only the most general characteristics of tea, and we encourage you to be much more poetic in your own descriptions. It is not uncommon for us to name other foods, beverages, or even chemical compounds when we taste tea and need a point of reference. The phrase "like sucking on a peach pit" is a favorite expression when we are tasting first-flush Darjeelings. We have also been known to refer to fresh-cut grass or spinach when cupping green teas.

Perhaps the most important part of the cupping experience is writing down your impressions. For the most experienced tasters in the world, it is their ability to recall previously tasted teas that sets them apart from others. Keep a small notebook and a pen handy when you are cupping. Besides helping you refine your tea-tasting vocabulary, it will also provide you with a lifeline to fond tea memories.

Finding Great Tea

All of the knowledge presented thus far—what is tea, where is it grown, the meaning of TGFOP, and the skills of cupping—have all been leading to this very crucial part of the book: helping you find great teas. You might have been a passionate consumer before you ever learned the meaning of first flush, but, with these newly acquired tools, you have more than passion—you have knowledge. You may, in fact, have more knowledge than many of your tea vendors.

Finding a source for consistently superb teas isn't an easy task in a world full of mocha-latte-blended drinks. Making the assumption that your local coffee roaster/retailer carries tea is logical, but no guarantee of great tea. The sad truth is that tea is often the red-headed stepchild in coffee stores. It is not an uncommon scenario to find a passionate coffee retailer operating his business under the banner of John Doe's Coffee & Tea, selling fresh-roasted whole beans from exotic estates, and offering you, the tea lover, a stale bag of tea from a company familiar to all because of its visible location on the grocery-store shelf.

"But wait," you may declare, "there are all of these new afternoon teahouses in my neighborhood!" These owner/operator businesses are passionate about incorporating the pleasures of tea into everyday life. While we applaud the growth of businesses that increase and endorse the enjoyment of tea, we have to stress that most of them place the emphasis on enjoyment and consider tea second.

This said, there are a number of businesses in both of these categories that care passionately about their tea and that are committed to bringing their customers the freshest, highest-quality teas from around the world. There are also emerging teahouses devoted solely to the leaf and mail-order resources with rare teas and a wealth of information. The information you glean from this book and, more important, from your own experiences, will help you to evaluate possible sources for great tea. As a point of reference, begin by comparing the traditional and consistent blends or origins from some of the more established sources. Then, use the following chart to rate potential resources.

Rating your Tea Source

Raise your teacup to them if:

- They offer no more than 50 teas. It is tempting for a retailer to offer literally hundreds of teas, because the selection of teas in the world is almost incomprehensible in its depth and breadth. We find that having 250 teas usually comes at the expense of freshness. Far better is the retailer who has a rotation of teas in and out of his store and turns them over quickly. If you are looking at six different first-flush Darjeelings and it's Christmas, well . . .
- Tea has an obvious place in their store. A variety of packaging options, tea accessories, and literature is prominently displayed.
- They offer freshly brewed pots of tea, and they take the time and effort necessary to do it correctly.
- The tea selection includes estate names as well as origins.

- Staff is obviously educated about the product or, better yet, passionate about it.
- The prices on the teas are in line with similar offerings from other vendors.

Raise an eyebrow and take your china cup elsewhere if:

- There is a tea menu akin in size to the Oxford English Dictionary.
- You find the tea section is two dusty shelves hidden behind small housewares.
- Their idea of tea service is a prepacked tea bag and water poured directly from the coffee urn or espresso machine.
- There is an overpowering aroma of cinnamon, peaches, mango, or any other flavoring.
- Staff is unable to answer any questions, or give useful information about tea.
- They proudly advertise paying more (and charging more) for their "rare and exotic" teas than anyone else. Great teas do *not* have to be expensive.

Bringing Your Discovery Home

When it comes to basic handling philosophies, tea is a lot like coffee. It shares the same enemies: oxygen, time, moisture, and heat. But, unlike coffee, tea is shelf-stable. What does this mean?

To begin with, tea, like coffee, should be stored in an airtight container, one that limits exposure to oxygen and moisture. Tea tins are traditional and still prevalent for a reason—they work. Storage containers for tea should be metal or at least an inert material. Be careful with plastics which can impart a chemical taste and aroma to tea, especially softer plastics like zipper bags. Glass or ceramic containers work well, but only if they are opaque, since exposure to light also speeds the staling process. Like coffee, tea should be stored away from moisture and heat. Because coffee is a seed and tea is a leaf, they have very different tolerances for things like temperature changes. Coffee has the hard protective shell of a seed, and because it has a more rigid cellular structure, it can naturally withstand certain external pressures better than tea. So, no temperature extremes, no refrigeration, and no freezing. Also, flavored teas must be kept meticulously separate from straight varietal or origin teas. Suppose you have a spicy cinnamon blend you just love for the holidays, and you store this alongside Assams, Fancy Formosa Oolongs, and Sencha. Well, you had better like this tea, because, within a few weeks, the *only* tea you will have will be spicy cinnamon blend, but in three different base teas!

By now you might be considering a humidity-controlled vault for your full-leaf treasures or you might be thinking that you can't possibly enjoy such a demanding product. Here's the good news. If you take simple precautions against oxygen, light, heat, and moisture you can keep great teas tasting great for months. Unlike coffee, which, even under the best conditions begins to stale hours after roasting, most tea remains stable for six months to a year. A professional may taste flavor loss sooner, but even a discerning consumer will be hard pressed in a black tea to detect staling for up to a year. And, as we said before, bad tea is quietly offensive. Stale tea doesn't change flavor as much as it loses flavor, becoming "papery" or "flat."

Tea Accouterments

Before getting too much into the accouterments of tea, we must confess that tea is simple. You *need* very few items to successfully steep and enjoy the world's finest teas. However, tea is also delightfully complex. It is a variety of beverages: traditional blends, new-age herbal infusions, fanciful flavored iced teas, and so on. Tea is also a formalized meal complete with its own etiquette. Finally, for many of us, tea is a personal statement about how one chooses to approach life. And one of the truly wonderful things about tea is all the neat stuff you can purchase to go with it: a seemingly endless variety of teapots, strainers, tea balls, fine porcelain cups and saucers, linens, and so on.

Today, with current interest in tea running high, the list of tea paraphernalia is not just long, but increasingly obscure: tea-themed paper goods, cookbooks, jewelry, t-shirts, to name only a few possibilities.

We spent a lot of time trying to decide what to cover in a short review of tea accessories. Which of these avenues to pursue: tea as simple, elegant, timeless beverage or tea as a retailer's cross-merchandising dream. We finally decided to list those items that we find to be essential, educational, or simply too seductive to pass up.

BREWING ACCOUTERMENTS

A Teakettle

We have more than a passing fondness for our electric teakettle. While there is something very homey and comforting about putting the kettle on, the innovation and convenience of an electric tea kettle make it top of our must-have list. It boils quickly, it's cordless, so we never knock over our samples with a loose cord, and, best of all, its heating element is entirely enclosed to prevent the buildup of those nasty lime deposits. Finally, it is stunning to look at, very modern, sleek, and sexy.

A Scale

It's not romantic, lovely to look at, or fun to use, but it is absolutely essential. We use a digital gram scale, which is dear enough that we carry it in our personal effects when traveling. It is accurate to 1/10 of a gram and is essential for achieving a consistent quality cup of tea.

A Timer

This may be the most important item in our tea brewing inventory, because, when we don't use it, we invariably end up drinking oversteeped, bitter, nasty tea. Ours is a handy little digital number with a mounting magnet.

A Teapot

This category is so multivaried and immense that we can't even begin to cover it. But we will be honest and tell you that we often brew black teas in a French press, and green and oolong teas in an absolutely fabulous little device called the Tea One brewer. French presses can be found in any cookware store, coffee house, or the kitchen department of nationwide retail stores. The Tea One Brewer is harder to find and harder to explain. Its shape is similar to a French Press, but it has two completely separate chambers. The upper chamber holds the tea and hot water and then, with the press of a small button, the tea empties into the bottom chamber and the top insert is lifted out and set aside. It makes a great cup of tea fun to brew.

Tea Cozy

When you are brewing a pot that is expected to sit for any length of time, a cozy is a handy way to keep your tea hot. Heaven forbid you leave tea on a hot plate, when cozies offer a colorful and efficient way of keeping the warmth in without "cooking" your tea. We even have them for our French Press.

Cups

For black teas taken with milk or sweeteners, we like a heavier cup and often use mugs. For the more delicate greens and oolongs, we prefer fine porcelain and use a set of handleless cups with saucers. Obviously your own tastes will dictate your drinking vessel.

EDUCATIONAL ACCOUTERMENTS

Tasting Sets

These aren't for drinking tea but for tasting it, and, when you're in the business, there is a big difference between the two. These three piece sets with a tasting pot, lid, and cupping bowl serve as a valuable tool in evaluating the infused leaf and liquor of teas you are interested in purchasing. We keep a minimum of 10 sets on hand. We liken owning a set (or three) of these to having a set of wine tasting glasses. No, they aren't essential, but they can certainly enhance the experience.

Literature

Our most-used volumes are listed in the bibliography, but we strongly believe in owning as many tea books as space and finances will allow. There isn't a single piece of literature out there that can capture every nuance of this beverage. There are books on tea's history, on the serving of afternoon tea, tea recipes, and many fine resources on buying, drinking, and enjoying the beverage.

Finally, here are the tea accessories we own for more than their intrinsic value. We think they are must-haves because of their beauty or use as conversation pieces.

Yixing Teapots

They are addictive. And, this is perhaps our most embarrassing confession—that, while we have enjoyed many great cups of tea brewed in Yixing pots, we have never used our own for that purpose. As some small measure of our atonement for this oversight, we offer here directions for using Yixing teapots. Yixing is a necessity for enjoying tea brewed Gong Fu style, where several infusions are made and enjoyed from tiny Yixing cups. Our own small collection of Yixing is arranged throughout the office and adds an elegant and exotic flair to the otherwise mundane setting.

How to Season Your Yixing Teapot

Yixing teapots are handmade from a particular clay found mostly in the Yi Xing region of China.

Although the clay comes in many colors, its most common is a dark brown with purple undertones; it is commonly referred to as *Purple Sand* clay. Very porous and absorbent, pots made with this clay can absorb the flavor of your tea during brewing. For this reason, it is suggested that you use only one type of tea with each pot. With continuous usage, the absorbed flavor will actually enhance your tea-brewing experience. Some families' teapots have been in use for decades, and rumor has it that they simply need to pour hot water into the pot to produce a fine cup of tea.

New Yixing pots may have an earthy or muddy taste, so you need to season the pot prior to using it. Begin by placing the entire pot, lid off, into a pot of clean, boiling water for 15 minutes. Remove and let dry completely, then submerge the pot into very strongly brewed tea for 6 to 8 hours. Do not cover the tea or expose to sunlight during this time. Remove the pot, let it air dry completely, and it is ready to use. *Never* use detergent for cleaning your pot. *Always* remove tea leaves after use, rinse with clear water, and let air dry.

(*Source:* Roy Fong, Imperial Tea Room, San Francisco, California)

Tea Brick

This pressed and imprinted brick made from tea leaves is also educational. It provides a visual presentation of tea's historical importance in the world of commerce. (Tea bricks were used as currency for bartering purposes.) And, with the addition of some yak butter and hot water, you could have an authentic Tibetan version of tea.

An Assortment of Pots, Strainers, Spoons, Spoon Rests, and More

While we own a large number of these items, they are usually only used for display. We keep promising that we will one day be organized and inspired enough to put on a true afternoon tea and give these lovely items their due, but, alas, the business of tea keeps us pretty busy.

Your tea accessories and collectibles should be an expression of you and your own experience of tea. Our eclectic tea things reflect our tastes in tea. We may begin the day with a hearty cup of Assam poured from a sturdy Brown Betty teapot but, by late afternoon, we are enjoying a delicately flavored and highly aromatic oolong from our Tea One brewer. Just as our taste in teas changes from day to day and hour to hour, our favorite accouterment changes to match.

Home Tea Brewers: The Problem Is Plastic

There are a number of electric home tea brewers on the market today. They are all serviceable enough and certainly make brewing loose tea more convenient. They do share some substantial drawbacks, and you should consider whether these outweigh convenience for you or whether convenience is king.

- *Plastic.* All of the home units that we have seen are manufactured to a large degree from molded plastic. While this makes them lighter and less expensive, it has the rather unsettling effect of contributing a distinctive plastic note to the brewed tea. We have had some success in eliminating this by repeatedly "curing" the brewers with very strong solutions of brewed tea for several hours, dramatically diminishing the presence of plastic flavors.
- *Hot water.* None of the home brewers we have used has managed to keep the water hot enough to do a good job steeping tea. The closest we have gotten is with the Chef's Choice Tea Mate, with an average temperature of about 205°F when steeping begins.

- *Room to grow.* Infusing tea leaves need lots of space in which to expand. All of the home brewers we tried were a little short on elbow room for the leaves to grow in.
- *Hot plates.* All of the tea brewers we tested had a hot plate designed to keep the carafe of brewed tea hot. This is fine if you are disciplined enough to throw out hot tea, but the temptation is great to leave the tea on the hot plate, and, after twenty minutes, the quality of the beverage decreases dramatically.

CHAPTER 5

Tea Blending

Some teas possess unique characteristics that make them ideal for consumption in their pure state. Others offer an excellent balance of color, brightness, and weight that yields a complex cup and an interesting or unique liquor. These teas, although not rare, are certainly not common. In the tea trade, we refer to them as *self-drinkers*. There are any number of teas that possess positive characteristics but come up short overall. These teas lend themselves to blending.

The goal of tea blending is to achieve one of two outcomes. The first is to create a blend in which the whole is greater than the sum of the parts. This is a task that is not easily achieved. Often, what would appear to be an ideal marriage of two or more teas results in a cacophony of discordant notes or a pale and listless brew that is considerably less palatable than any of its parents. Thus, a truly exceptional blend is a rare accomplishment.

The second, much more common, and, generally more successful, objective in blending is to create a tea with a particular flavor profile that can endure through frequent substitution of one component for another. This blending arises out of necessity, as there are finite, and sometimes very small, quantities of certain teas available each year. Most medium-to-large tea concerns will blend to establish a flavor profile, and then work with a wide variety of different teas to maintain that flavor. This enables the tea purveyor to maintain a consistent cup of tea from season to season and year to year.

This approach to blending may cover a wide variety of origins or may be confined to a small region within a given origin. For example, a small quantity of BOP teas from each of several Darjeeling gardens might be blended to produce a tea that is clearly a Darjeeling tea, but which cannot be identified as the produce of any one garden. Conversely, a tea purveyor might blend teas from China, India, Ceylon, and Kenya, from a large selection of gardens and co-operatives, to produce a distinctive flavor. Here the art of blending becomes a science. Tasters who have developed a vast sensory memory are employed to sample from an enormous array of teas and then to create constantly changing formulas that are consistent with the original flavor profile. One tea may be added for its color, another for its weight, and yet another for its brightness. As available supplies of one tea are consumed, one or more replacements are added to the melange, and others may drop out.

Botanical Ingredients and Flavorings

Tea also has a long tradition of being blended with other botanical ingredients. Ginger, onions, salt, jasmine flowers, rose petals, and lychee nuts have all found their way into tea blends, and some have become recognized standards that are appreciated by tea lovers around the world.

In addition to botanical additives, there are a great many flavorings that have been applied to tea. These range from natural extracts of fruits and berries to a vast array of nature identical, natural and artificial, and wholly synthetic flavors. The majority of these are in liquid form and are aerosolized and sprayed onto tea leaves. The flavored leaves are then tumbled to homogenize the flavoring and then left to rest for a period of time. Flavorings are available from a vast array of suppliers, in liquid and dry forms, in a variety of solvent agents, and in natural, artificial, natural and artificial (N&A), nature identical, and natural with other natural flavors (WONF). For the home tea blender, we suggest that you stick with blending already-flavored teas. Many flavoring companies produce flavors specifically for tea, and most will recommend a dosage for application to tea, but none we know of will sell flavor in a quantity that makes home flavoring logistically possible.

Origin teas alone represent an incredible range of flavors and aromas, but, when all of the possibilities for blending and flavoring are taken into account, the potential taste profiles are too numerous to count.

Creating Your Own Personal Masterpiece

If you have an interest in blending teas on your own, whether merely for the sake of curiosity or to try to develop a unique signature blend, there are some basic points to consider. First, and foremost, you should gain adequate experience in tasting origin teas to have developed a solid sensory memory of the inherent flavor characteristics of a variety of teas. Second, you should prepare yourself emotionally. The single most common mistake that novice blenders make is the loss of objectivity. It seems perfectly natural that a certain sense of pride and paternalism occurs when tasting a tea that is the result of your own blending efforts. It is sometimes difficult to be an unbiased judge of the relative merits of this new little creation that bears your stamp. Strive for objectivity in assessing the success of your blending efforts. Try to judge accurately whether your blend represents a total flavor profile that is actually better than any of the component parts.

Blending Methodology

Here is a simple procedure for blending that should be useful for gaining practice in the art.

1. Acquire sufficient quantities of a variety of origin teas to experiment with. At a minimum, about 100 grams should do.

2. Taste all of the teas at least once on their own, making notes of the leaf size and style, the aroma, the flavor, the mouth feel, and any-outstanding characteristics. (For best results, use the standard cupping practices discussed in Chapter 5.)

3. Commit to paper some thoughts about what the desired result will be like, and create a few blending recipes that look good on paper. For example, you may want to create a very intensely flavored Irish Breakfast blend. Identify teas from your available library of samples that may have characteristics you associate with a good Irish Breakfast tea.

4. Prepare a brewed sample of a number of the teas that you have selected as potential candidates for your blend, as well as a few that you find interesting for their own sake.

5. Use a spoon to draw off some of the brewed teas into a cup, starting with one-to-one blends of just two types, and sample the result. Using this method, you can extend the number of tea types and adjust ratios as you go. Keep good notes on both the makeup and results of these liquid blends.

6. When you have arrived at some blend of the liquid teas that interests you, try blending the dry tea leaves at or near the same ratios. It is best to let the dry blends sit for a day or two before tasting them, as the flavors tend to meld and change for some time. (An important note when blending leaf teas—look for leaves that are sufficiently similar in size and density to ensure that the teas will remain well blended. Very fine leaves may settle out of the blend if mixed with larger, coarser, leaf styles.)

7. If the blend continues to show promise, check all your previous tasting notes and, if necessary, make adjustments to the blend. If adjustments are made, repeat step 6.

8. It is important to keep good notes throughout the process, and to refer to them frequently. When your available supply of the component teas is exhausted, you will probably need to repeat much of the original ex-

ercise in order to ensure that any replacement teas continue to work well in the blend. Remember, tea is an agricultural product, and many of its characteristics will change from season to season, influenced by weather, processing, storage, and age. Don't be afraid to reformulate your favorite blend. Trust your palate, and blend to the distinctive flavor profile you have created.

This methodology will not guarantee you success. It will help you to get a sense of the likely results of your efforts without constantly mixing and, ultimately, discarding dry blends.

If you are interested in adding other elements, like botanical ingredients, it is important that you not only know what any single ingredients may taste like when brewed, but that you have a sound knowledge of their provenance and are well aware of their impact on the human body.

Botanical ingredients are available in a wide variety of sizes, shapes, and grades, and may include flowers, berries, bark, seeds, roots, and even pollens. Many yield unique colors and flavors when brewed, and can enhance both the appearance and taste of a tea blend or tisane.

The best reason for blending at home is that it will help you develop sensory memory of a variety of tea tastes. Finally, it can be a tremendous amount of fun. So, start brewing, blending, and enjoying!

CHAPTER 6

The Agony of the Leaves: Preparing Tea at Home

When you are steeping tea for professional analysis, watching the reaction of the dried leaves as water is poured over them is referred to as "the agony of the leaves." It's a poetic expression and a truly beautiful thing to watch, especially in the larger-leafed teas such as oolong. In fact, we often brew in clear vessels for the sheer visual impact of this display. Besides being poetic and aesthetically pleasing, this interaction between water and leaves can tell you a lot about your particular tea: how fresh it is, and what care was taken in its processing.

These days, unfortunately, the introduction of water to tea can be called the agony of the leaves for less than poetic reasons. Oh, the agony of those poorly extracted, overly steeped and often tightly confined leaves. Worse yet is the agony of the tea drinker who is forced to drink the liquor acquired from them.

So, what goes wrong in the preparation of tea? Is brewing an art form, whose mastery requires an indulgent muse or a sacrifice to some heretofore unnamed tea god? Or is proper tea brewing the product of militant practice? Zenlike calm? Modern technological wonders? Really, it's none of the above.

"And a Spoon for the Pot": Proper Traditional Steeping

The most commonly cited obstacles to serving really wonderful tea brewed from loose leaves are that it is complicated or too time consuming. The truth is that brewing tea requires hot water, tea, and a vessel in which to bring the two together. If you have these things—fire, water, tea, vessel—then you can have tea. You may not have the absolutely perfectly brewed, choirs of angels singing, Fourth of July fireworks experience that is possible with tea, but you will certainly have a drinkable beverage. In fact, for thousands of years, wise men have been pouring hot water over the leaves of the *Camellia sinensis* bush and finding pleasure in both the experience and the resultant beverage.

But, what if you want a tea epiphany when you sip your oolong? Then you need a couple of other items, namely, time and patience. Truly great tea cannot be hurried. Or, put another way, the path to great tea is paved with gram scales and water-filtration devices. Do not despair; great tea is worth the educational journey, and, once you learn a few simple rules, brewing the perfect cup can be quite simple. The result is a beverage with distinctive and exceptional flavors, aromas, and colors.

Rule No. 1. Brewing Tea Is a Weighty Exercise

A standard cup of tea is not an 8 ounce cup but, like a cup of coffee, 5.5 liquid ounces. So, the first step in correctly brewing a great cup of tea is to know the liquid capacity of your preferred teapot. The capacity of your brewing vessel determines how much tea you should use. The general rule of thumb is to use 2 grams of tea leaves for each cup (5.5 liquid ounces) of water. Because tea leaves vary widely in size, shape, and weight, it is difficult to translate 2 grams into a volumetric measure, such as a teaspoon. So, great brewing begins with a scale.

Our best advice is to take some time and use an accurate gram scale along with an adjustable measuring spoon. Compare weights to volume, and determine what two grams of the tea you are considering looks like in your spoon. The rest is math; if your tea takes one and one half teaspoons to make two grams, and you are using an 11-ounce tea pot, then you will need three teaspoons of tea to produce a pot. It may sound complicated at first, but you will get the hang of it quickly. We recommend that, once you have discovered the right measure, you record it. We make a thumbnail drawing of the amount of tea needed (with a heaping, scant, or level teaspoon) on inexpensive white labels and put them on the top of our tea canisters. This saves having to reinvent the wheel each time and makes measurement so easy that even our two older boys can measure out a pot of tea.

RULE NO. 2. BOILING IS NOT ALWAYS BEST

Most tea drinkers, even the true neophytes, have heard that, to produce a great cup of tea, you need to bring your water to a rolling boil. The rule is so well-known and respected that it almost seems as irrefutable as Newton's Law in physics. So, are we about to commit an act of tea heresy in proclaiming that boiling is not always best? No, because this rule has saved many a cup of *black* tea from well-intentioned brewers who would pour water from their coffee maker over tea and expect a flavorful beverage. The fresh, boiling water rule is important, and its widespread use cannot be faulted, because it adheres to the KISS rule (Keep It Simple, Stupid). We are willing to go out on a limb, though, and believe that, if you are in love with tea enough to read a book on the subject, then you are willing to allow for more complexity in your beverage's needs and embrace that complexity when it appears in its taste.

Why is boiling not always best? Tea is produced in three distinct styles: black, oolong, and green. (see Chapter 1) Each of these styles has different water temperature guidelines for steeping. For black teas, water should absolutely be brought to a rolling boil (212°F) before it is poured. For oolong teas, the water temperature should be slightly cooler (195°F–210°F), depending on the degree of oxidation in the particular oolong. Green teas require cooler water still (180°F)—an effect that can be achieved by carrying the water to the tea instead of the tea to the water. Water cools rapidly enough that the journey from heat source to table will result in a drop in temperature. This is a rather clinical approach to the water temperature. Japanese texts on tea brewing contain haiku and poetic metaphors that aptly describe the same reality; the correct water temperature is imperative for great tea.

Rule No. 3. Know What's in the Water

A cup of tea is a tiny bit of tea, and a whole lot of water. Knowing what is in the water you use is critical to producing a great-tasting cup. Historically, teahouses in China and the United States were often located next to wells, and it was common knowledge that the water from these special places was what made the tea stand out. Today you can still find evidence of "water prejudice." It has been said that Seattle water is one of the best for brewing tea, and many Chinese still insist that spring water makes the best cup. Should you not live next to a freshwater spring, or near the Space Needle, what do you look for in good water?

First and foremost, you want to be able to clearly taste the tea, so no strong aromas or tastes can be present. If you do have highly chlorinated or earthy-tasting water, there are numerous water filtration devices which can remove off-flavors or aromas, or you can use bottled water when you are brewing. But, aside from bad flavors or disruptive aromas, there are also mineral components in water, like calcium, which can contribute to or distract from the tea's flavor. The amount of oxygen in the water can also be a factor in the final cup. Water that has set overnight in a boiler will make a flat, lifeless cup of tea; hence, you should always fill your kettle with freshly drawn water.

Today, we are happy to be helping our friends at Water Systems Group and the American Premium Tea Institute create scientific standards for tea water. David Beeman and Martin Swanson at Water Systems Group have perfected devices that allow us to tweak the amount of TDS (total dissolved solids) in our tea water and further allow us to control what minerals are present in those solids. Although we still don't have a scientific formula for what makes the best tea water, we are joined by a cast of professional tasters who are forging the way for this formula to exist. For now, we know that 35–50 TDS seems to be the most widely agreed-upon number for great tea. A total lack of dissolved minerals makes for weak aromatic and flavor components, so avoid distilled water. An over-abundance can muddy the liquor and can cause lighter floral notes to get lost.

The bottom line: Water should be fresh, clean, and odorless. If you wouldn't think of drinking it out of the tap, don't use it to make your tea.

Rule No. 4. Time Is of the Essence

It is almost impossible to give steeping times for tea down to the second, because extraction is invariably a matter of taste, and taste is always subjective. However, nothing is worse in our opinion than an over-steeped cup of tea. The bitterness is extraordinary. It usually makes you feel as if your teeth have been stripped of all porcelain. To avoid this awful feeling, we keep timers in the places where we steep tea, and we use them fanatically. How many minutes do we set the timers for? We wish we could tell you five minutes and stop there, but, of course, we can't.

While there are some general guidelines, steeping times vary according to the tea's color, style, and grade. Here are some general parameters in relation to leaf size: full, large-leafed teas like high-grade oolongs can take additional time, because they have less surface area in contact with the water and extraction is slower; smaller-leaf teas like Hao Ya Keemun will take less; and the CTC teas used in tea bags are designed for maximum surface area exposure and require very little time to create a dark (dare I say, foreboding) cup of tea.

Regarding differences in process, for black teas, steeping times are between three to five minutes; for Oolong teas, steeping times are four to seven minutes; for green teas, steeping times are around two to three minutes. Other important steeping guidelines include herbal teas at five to seven minutes; delicate white teas at around two minutes; and First Flush Darjeeling teas at two to five minutes. Again, these are guidelines only and personal taste should have the final word on how long to extract specific teas. Many an Irish grandmother likes to stand her spoon up in her tea. We strongly believe that the best way to drink tea is the way you like it. Experiment!

Perhaps the most important thing to remember for those seeking to brew great tea is that tea requires its devotees to take time. Take the time to learn about how you like your tea, and then take time to steep it and to drink it and, one day, you will realize that you are making the perfect cup . . . for you.

America's Cup: Iced Tea

Americans have always had a knack for product development. Or, put another way, we love to be different. No wonder that while the rest of the world drinks their tea hot, we are busy consuming 80 percent or more of our tea on ice, and the thirst for iced tea doesn't seem to be diminishing. There are many reasons for iced tea's continuing growth; here are a couple of them.

The Birth of a National Beverage

It was 1904 at the World's Fair in St. Louis, Missouri, and Mr. Richard Blechynden, an English promotor hired by an association of India tea growers, was having a bad day. He had created a fantastic booth, staffed with excrutiatingly polite and exotically turbaned Indian servants, and he was serving delicious cups of piping hot tea. Unfortunately, he had failed to take into account that summer in the midwest is much closer in temperature to New Delhi than Stratford-on-Avon. His customers were few, his job was on the line, and his discomfort was increasing exponentially. Whether in a fit of marketing genius or in sheer desperation for something cool to drink, he poured the black teas over ice and created a beverage sensation. His midwestern drinkers (tried and true green-tea fanatics at the time) tried the refreshing drink and, thus, was born a market that today is close to $3 billion.

ICED IS EASY

Perhaps the biggest reason that iced tea is such booming business is that, unlike hot tea, iced tea is foodservice friendly. Convenience does seem to be the passport to success with the U. S. consumer. Equipment companies have iced-tea brewers, which require minimal manual dexterity and intellectual power. Pull out the brew basket, place the filter-bag of tea inside, return the basket, push a button. This is great news for most foodservice operators, whose staff tend to spend more time worrying about the prom than about how much tea is needed to make a gallon. For the consumer, it means a consistent, quality product. Iced tea is also easy to produce at home; for pointers on a great cup of iced tea see the accompanying box.

Trade Secrets to Great Iced Tea

Start with good (not great) tea. China black, South Indian, and Ceylon teas seem to do the best job for iced tea. Many of the China black teas have the added advantage of very low creaming temperatures, which translates to crystal-clear iced tea. Experiment with blends and flavored teas to find the ones you like best.

- Brew a double-strength concentrate to start. Use one ounce of whole-leaf tea for each quart of water just off the boil. Let steep for three to five minutes, then strain out the tea leaves.
- Dilute the concentrate with an equal amount of room-temperature water, or more to taste. Avoiding the quick change from hot to cold also seems to prevent clouding.
- Pour over ice and enjoy. Cover and refrigerate any remaining tea but, in any event, use it all or discard it within 24 hours.
- If you like your tea sweetened, add sugar before dilution, while the tea is still very hot. This will help the sugar to stay dissolved in the tea.

Stay out of the Sun

We hate to put a damper on what seems to be an American tradition, but we recommend strongly against making sun tea. One of the great built-in safety features of tea is that it is traditionally made with boiled water, which serves to kill any organisms in water, as well as sterilize the tea leaves. While tea is generally not a good host for microorganisms in its dry state, it is a haven for bacteria after it has been brewed and cooled. Leaving your tea out in the sun is somewhat akin to leaving a steak on the counter overnight. Furthermore, studies done at the University of Miami link kidney stones to tea consumption, with the interesting finding that sun tea might be the culprit. It seems that the extended steeping time of the sun-tea process brings out components of the tea that might aid in kidney-stone formation.

VARIETY ON ICE

Perhaps nowhere else in the world of tea have we run into so many unique flavors. There are the tried and true tropical flavors like passion fruit and mango, which paved the way for the orchard flavors like raspberry and peach. In today's market, there is no limit to the flavors you will find on ice: vanilla, bergamot, ginger, and grapefruit, to name a few. Beyond the ever-expanding variety of flavors, there is something even better happening for iced tea: Flavor differentiation due to a greater variety of base teas. It was a relief when this category saw the emergence of good black teas for a base, but now there are iced teas with Sencha, Gunpowder, and specific-origin black teas available. Add a healthy dose of herbal components to the mix and things really get exciting. Not only is the glass of tea you're drinking delicious and refreshing, but now it can have medicinal properties as well!

MESSAGE IN A BOTTLE

Yet another advantage of iced tea is its ability to fit nicely into a bottle, can, or other container. I'm not talking corn syrup and flavored water here, but real tea. The chemical construct of tea is such that it can be a shelf-stable product without the addition of chemical preservatives or stabilizers and their consequent impact on flavor and health. Just as beer saw a revolution (led by microbrewers across the country) against the bland products of large commercial breweries, so too has ready-to-drink iced tea seen the advent of better and more interesting products, crafted by small companies with a passion for their products. In fact, a number of exciting bottled-tea products are being produced jointly with beer microbrewers!

CHAPTER 7

Enjoying Fine Tea

Tea is an ancient beverage, second only to water in terms of world consumption, so it is no surprise that many rituals and traditions surround the enjoyment of it as a beverage. From the profoundly and intrinsically spiritual Japanese tea ceremony, to the soothing social occasion of afternoon tea, which some may reasonably argue can become a spiritual event, tea is one item whose consumption is as fascinating as its flavor. We present highlights from these two very different perspectives, because we see an increasing awareness of, and curiosity about, them emerging alongside the increasing popularity of tea. We also give you a few recipes to enjoy with tea or, for the truly adventurous tea lovers, recipes that include tea in their ingredients.

The Japanese Tea Ceremony

The most evolved of all the ceremonies and rituals surrounding tea is certainly the Japanese tea ceremony, the *Cha No Yu*, or hot water for tea. This ceremony represents the culmination of the Japanese elevation of tea from a medicine or beverage to a way of life, a religion of aestheticism. In his 1906 work, *The Book of Tea*, Kakuzo Okakura describes this philosophy, *teaism*, thus:

> *Teaism is a cult founded on the adoration of the beautiful among the sordid facts of everyday existence. It inculcates purity and harmony, the mystery of mutual charity, the romanticism of the social order. It is essentially a worship of the Imperfect, as it is a tender attempt to accomplish something possible in this impossible thing we know as life.*

The ceremony is practiced today all over the world, and, even if you do not intend to embrace tea as a philosophy or religion, there is a real beauty in this practice and much to be learned from it. The ritual traditionally is held in a *Sukiya*, or tea room, which is designed along rigid traditional lines, originally described by Sho-O, a fifteenth century tea master. The freestanding tea room as is often found today was created by Rikyu, regarded by practitioners of the art as the greatest tea master of all time. The tea room is intended to be quite plain, reflecting the virtues of poverty and simplicity.

Upon arriving at the Sukiya, guests are first stationed in the portico, or *machiai,* until they are summoned to enter. From the machiai, they pass along the *roji,* or garden path, to the tea room proper. Here, tradition calls for those bearing arms to hang their swords outside, embracing the peace of the tea room. The door is a mere three feet in height, forcing all who enter to bow very low to pass through. This is designed to reinforce humility, as all must assume a very small stature for the ceremony.

The area in which the ceremony is performed is tiny, only ten feet by ten feet. The guests arrive and take a few moments to appreciate the arranged room, taking in the traditional scroll, the fire, the kettle, and any other utensils that are displayed. In a few moments, they are greeted individually by the host, who then returns to the preparation room to prepare the *kaiseki,* a small meal. After the meal, the host adds fresh fuel to the fire, and a sweet is served. At this point, the guests may retire to the garden, waiting for a gong to summon them for the tea, or they may stay in place in the tea room.

The practice of the *Cha No Yu* highlights cleanliness and hygiene, and this is evident in the preparation of the tea. Each utensil is ceremonially wiped clean, and the exaggerated movements of the tea master are carefully choreographed. A thick tea is served first; the host may prepare and serve a thin tea afterwards. The host will engage the guests in conversation, and they will admire the utensils and decor. Finally, the host will bid the guests good-bye, and stand in the doorway until they are out of sight.

The Seven Rules of Rikyu

The great tea master Rikyu summed up the entirety of the tea ceremony in seven seemingly simple rules. Their simplicity belies the difficulty of adhering to them strictly, and they remain the guiding principles for today's practitioners.

1. Make a delicious bowl of tea.
2. Lay the charcoal so that it heats the water.
3. Arrange the flowers as they are in the field.
4. In summer suggest coolness; in winter, warmth.
5. Do everything ahead of time.
6. Prepare for rain.
7. Give those with whom you find yourself every consideration.

Since the time of Rikyu, the tea ceremony has been practiced, studied, and constantly refined by those who embrace the philosophy. The tea and the ritual are finally secondary to the study and practice. To the uninitiated, it is merely a beautiful ceremony, but to those who follow the way of tea, *Chado*, it represents a path towards an enlightened life.

For an opportunity to learn more about the tea ceremony and the tea life, contact the Urasenke Foundation. They have offices in Kyoto, Japan, New York, and San Francisco, as well as other cities in the United States and around the world. Urasenke carries on the traditional teachings of Rikyu, and the grand tea master is a fifteenth generation descendant of his. We strongly recommend that any lover of tea witness this exceptional ritual at least once. It is, as the Urasenke Foundation says, "a ritual of simplicity and economy wherein all can find 'peace in a bowl of tea.' "

Afternoon Tea

Anna, the seventh Duchess of Bedford, was a woman unwilling to accept discomfort, and thank goodness for that. As was the custom in England in the 1700s, Anna would have a huge breakfast, a meal hardly worth calling lunch, and then wait until 8:00 P.M. or later before sitting down to a substantial dinner. Those of us who eat a snack at the computer and then rush off after work to pick up kids, dry cleaning, and groceries, and then begin cooking dinner at 7:00 P.M.

know exactly how Anna felt when she described this "sinking feeling" she got around 5 P.M.

In our modern and rather unimaginative times, we usually reach for a soda or a candy bar. How wonderful then for Anna to combat this lull in energy and spirit by sitting down to a nice cup of tea accompanied by sandwiches and cakes. The idea was such a good one that soon her acquaintances were joining her, and afternoon tea became a ritual and quite probably the most enjoyable part of the day.

Over time, this ritual of afternoon tea diversified and two very distinct versions came into being. *Low tea* quite contrary to its title was the showy, ostentatious, and rather less nutritious version of tea which was served in aristocratic homes. Here the emphasis was more on the china and linens than on the beverage or accompanying foods. No doubt this low tea is where the stiff pinky finger first began poking out from the side of teacups. *High tea* went to the other extreme, and was embraced by the middle class who served up whopping plates of food alongside a nice strong cuppa.

Whether high or low, afternoon tea became as much a social phenomenon as it was a culinary trend. Today's re-emerging interest in afternoon tea is also a social movement, a revolt against the high-voltage beverages and fast-paced living in which too many of us find ourselves enmeshed. The tea industry has found an important place in direct opposition to the to-go mentality of coffee bars. Unlike the quickly produced gratification of an espresso drink, teahouses are inviting their guests to partake in a more luxurious and languid joy.

The proliferation of teahouses and hotels serving afternoon tea not only is testimony to consumer's desire to indulge themselves but also speaks to the fact that America is looking for ways to connect with others in a setting that is healthy and apolitical. For business and social occasions, martini lunches are full of potential public-relations disasters. A typical trendy restaurant may offer safer haven, but you are also likely to deal with pompous staff and a high-decibel ambience. What safer bet than to have your future mother-in-law, new boss, or potential client to afternoon tea? It's so civilized. It's so soothing. It's so delicious!

If you have not experienced the joy of having efficient service, delectable food, and hushed conversation, then you must escape to an afternoon teahouse soon. While afternoon tea is not of the same stoically spiritual nature as the Japanese tea ceremony, there is still something calming and meditative in its ritualized service and comforting foods. As Henry James said in his novel *Portrait of a Lady*, "There are few hours in life more agreeable than the hour dedicated to the ceremony known as afternoon tea."

Shall I Pour? Ten Tips for Tea Etiquette

If you are going to sit down to a proper afternoon tea, it is only fitting that you do so with style. To prevent any faux pas at the tea table, we consulted with the nation's foremost expert on tea etiquette. The following ten tips were compiled from The Protocol School of Washington's founder and director, Dorothea Johnson. The school is the nation's leading etiquette and protocol firm, and Ms. Johnson is author of the *Little Book of Etiquette, Tea and Etiquette,* and *Outclass the Competition*. Ms. Johnson has trained and certified tea etiquette consultants throughout the United States and abroad. Many of them are featured on major television networks and in publications worldwide.

The Do's

Do rise, regardless of gender, to greet and shake hands with your guests.

Do wait until you have swallowed the food in your mouth before you take a sip of tea.

Do place your napkin on your chair when you briefly leave the table.

Do place your knife and fork in the 10:20 position when you have finished eating. Place the tips of the utensils at 10 and the handles at 4.

Do spread the scone with jam first and then cream.

The Don'ts

Don't place items on the table. This protocol extends to keys, hats, gloves, eyeglasses, eyeglass cases, anything that's not part of the meal.

Don't extend a pinkie when holding a cup. This is an outdated affectation.

Don't push your plate away from you at the end of the tea.

Don't place your napkin on the table until you're ready to leave.

Don't involve your guest(s) in paying the bill. The host bears sole responsibility for the bill.

(*Source:* Dorothea Johnson, The Protocol School of Washington)

Tea-Time Recipes

Afternoon tea is usually accompanied by a variety of light foods, including tiny finger sandwiches, fresh fruit or berries, petit fours or other small pastries, and, of course, light, fluffy scones served just warm with jam and clotted cream. Sandwiches are an area in which you can let your imagination run wild—from classics like thinly sliced cucumber to heartier smoked fish and meats. The key is to remember that everything is part of a light repast, and portions are meant to be diminutive. We have included a recipe for the most critical tea time item, scones, as well as a nice sweet bread that works well with tea.

The Peninsula Beverly Hills Currant Scones

This is our favorite scone in the world, and they are served daily, along with a delightful array of sandwiches, pastries, and petit fours, at The Peninsula Beverly Hills, California's most elegant hotel. They were created by the talented husband and wife team of Bill and Michelle Bracken. Bill is the Executive Chef at The Peninsula, and his wife is a pastry chef, now on a part-time basis, and a mother, on a full-time basis.

Yield: 27 scones

2 ⅔ c. all-purpose flour
2 ⅔ c. cake flour

4 tbs. baking powder
1 tsp. salt
½ c. sugar
two 4-oz. sticks butter
2 eggs
1 ¼ c. milk
1 ¼ c. cream
2 cups currants

1. Preheat oven to 450°.
2. Place all the dry ingredients in a large electric mixing bowl.
3. Add the wet ingredients and mix with a dough hook until just integrated.
4. Add the currants and mix for 30 seconds.
5. Remove from the bowl and hand knead for 1–2 minutes.
6. Flatten to 3/4" to 1" thick and cut in rounds.
7. Brush with eggwash and bake at 450° for approximately 15 minutes, or until golden brown.

Serve with your favorite preserves and clotted cream.

McCharles House Zucchini–Pistachio Tea Bread

Our friends Audrey and Vivian Heredia, a mother-daughter team, own the McCharles House Tea Room in Tustin, California. Their tea room is everything afternoon tea service should be: comforting, unhurried, and delicious. Although they don't part easily with recipes, we begged them for one of our favorites. This tea bread is a great accompaniment to any cup of tea.

Makes 1 loaf

1 ½ c. all-purpose flour
1 ½ tsps. baking soda
¼ tsp. ground cinnamon
¾ c. sugar
2 large eggs
½ c. vegetable oil
1 tsp. vanilla extract
½ tsp. salt
1 ½ c. grated zucchini, squeezed dry
1 ½ c. shelled toasted pistachio nuts

For the frosting:
1 large egg white
¾ c. sugar
2 ½ tbs. cold water
⅛ tsp. cream of tartar
¾ tsp. light corn syrup
½ tsp. vanilla extract

1. Preheat the oven to 350° F.
2. In a bowl, sift together the flour, baking soda, and cinnamon.
3. In another bowl, whisk together the sugar, eggs, vegetable oil, vanilla and salt. Add to the dry ingredients and stir until combined.
4. Fold in the zucchini and nuts.

5. Transfer the batter to a well-buttered 5 × 9 inch loaf pan and bake for 50–60 minutes, or until a cake tester inserted in the center comes out clean.
6. Let cool in the pan on a rack for 10 minutes. Invert onto the rack and cool completely.

To make the frosting:

7. In a double boiler set over simmering water, combine all ingredients except the vanilla. Using a hand mixer, beat the mixture for 7 minutes or until thick and fluffy. Beat in the vanilla.
8. Frost top of cake and allow frosting to set before serving.

Recipes with Tea

Chef Robert Wemischner is a magician when it comes to taking our favorite tea flavors and incorporating them into delicious recipes. Recipes for afternoon tea tend to be bound by tradition. Some may argue that putting currants in the scones is adventurous but, for the truly daring, we offer Chef Wemischner's creations. Following you will find an entree, a beverage and a dessert which take tea into a whole new world of exotic flavors and adventurous ingredients.

Smoked Chicken Salad with Tea Vinaigrette

Here a boldly flavored Chinese Yunnan tea is used in an oil-free dressing to add depth of flavor to this main-dish salad. Water chestnuts add crunch, and ripe pear and dried currants provide a sweet counterpoint to the smokiness of the chicken. If fresh, tiny, Champagne grapes are available, for an elegant touch, by all means substitute them for their dried brethren.

Yield: 4 lunch or light supper servings

The tea dressing:

1 Tbl. Yunnan black tea leaves
1 c. apple juice
1 tsp. Dijon-style mustard
½ c. buttermilk
Salt and freshly ground black pepper to taste

For the salad:

1 lb. smoked chicken breasts
1 c. water chestnuts, well drained and sliced
2 ripe but firm Bosc pears, peeled and slivered
1 c. dried currants, soaked in hot water for 5 minutes, and then drained

The assembly:

1 head butter lettuce, washed and dried well, or 1 small head Napa cabbage, thinly sliced

1. Make the dressing. Bring the apple juice to a boil. Add the tea leaves and let steep for about 5 minutes. Strain through fine sieve and place in a

bowl. Allow to cool. Blend the mustard and buttermilk and then gradually add the cooled apple-juice–infused tea. Add salt and pepper to taste. (I like this with a generous amount of black pepper.)

2. Slice the chicken into long thin strips. Combine with the water chestnuts, pears, currants. Coat with half of the dressing. Place on a bed of butter lettuce or shredded Napa cabbage. Pour remaining dressing over each salad and serve immediately.

ICED JASMINE TEA WITH LEMONGRASS SYRUP

Here, two powerful Asian flavors meet in a glass. Perfect when the weather heats up, this simple drink shows off the flowery quality of the best jasmine tea from the Fujian region of China. Here in the southeastern part of China, heat dried green tea leaves are layered at night with newly opened fragrant jasmine flowers plucked that morning. The subtle tang of lemongrass adds just the right edge of tartness.

Yield: 2 servings

The Lemongrass Syrup:

6 fat stalks of fresh lemongrass
2 c. granulated sugar
2 c. water
(Note: The above quantities will be enough to make plenty of syrup for other uses as well.)

The tea:

2 Tbl. jasmine tea
1 quart cold water

Garnishes:

1 stalk lemongrass
¼ of fresh pineapple, cored, thinly sliced into wedges

1. Make the syrup by bringing the sugar and water to boil. When boiling, add the lemongrass stalks, which have been coarsely chopped and mashed with a mallet or rolling pin to release their flavor. Remove from the heat and allow to stand until cool. Strain through a fine sieve. Pour into a glass jar, cover, and refrigerate. This will keep at least a month in the refrigerator and may also be used to flavor dressings, or drizzled over fresh starfruit, melon, pineapple, mango, papaya, or a combination of any or all of the preceding.
2. Brew the tea by heating water to 180–185° F. Allow to infuse for 3 minutes. Strain and reserve.
3. Pour about 1 tablespoon of the lemongrass syrup in each tall glass. Top with tea, add ice as desired. Garnish with a stick of lemongrass inserted into a thin wedge of fresh pineapple.

Green Tea-poached Asian Pears with Pistachio-Cream sauce, Edged with a Rumor of Mint

Here's a refreshing dessert with a touch of luxury that works year round. Its complex taste belies a simple method of preparation.

Yield: 4 Servings

4 Asian pears
1 c. granulated sugar
2 c. freshly brewed green tea
1 2" piece fresh gingerroot, peeled and sliced into thin coins
Peel half an average sized lemon
1 large sprig fresh mint

Garnish:

Fresh mint leaves, if desired

1. Peel the pears and core with a corer or a small paring knife, being sure to remove the tart center core area of each. Place the sugar, green tea, gingerroot, lemon peel and mint in a medium-size saucepan large enough to hold the four pears in a single layer. Over medium heat, bring the mixture to just under the boil, or until the sugar is fully dissolved. Reduce the heat to a simmer and add the peeled and cored pears. Cook for 15–20 minutes (the pears will remain firm). Allow to cool

to room temperature and then refrigerate, covered. Meanwhile make the Pistachio-Cream Sauce.

Pistachio-Cream Sauce:

1 c. nonfat plain yogurt, well drained
½ c. buttermilk
1 tsp. pure maple syrup
1 c. shelled and skinned pistachios (natural, no coloring), coarsely chopped

In a small bowl, whisk together the yogurt, buttermilk and maple syrup. Add the nuts and store mixture in refrigerator until serving time.

Assembly:

Just before serving, remove pears from poaching liquid, drain well and place one each in four chilled goblets. Mask with the sauce and serve immediately, garnished with fresh mint leaves, if desired.

CHAPTER 8

Tea and Health

The support for the benefits of various plant sources range from folklore, to anecdotal, to epidemiological, to hard scientific evidence. While we are all very excited about the potential of phytochemicals to enhance the quality of life and prevent chronic disease, we must be cautious not to over promise the public with prevention or cures that are not carefully documented and substantiated by carefully controlled clinical research.

—J. W. Finley, "Dietary Phytochemicals in Cancer Prevention & Treatment," *Advances in Experimental Biology & Medicine*, 1996

There has been a tremendous amount of excitement lately about the possible health benefits associated with the regular consumption of tea, particularly green tea. Some of the touted benefits include cancer prevention, cardiovascular health, antioxidant properties, and the prevention of tooth decay. While we would love to write that each of these benefits is a scientific fact, and that you should immediately begin consuming immense quantities of tea, our consciences forbid it. The most important thing to grasp in the tea and health argument is that these are *potential* benefits and that a great deal of additional research is necessary before there will be any conclusive evidence. It is our personal philosophy that our grandmothers were right when they said "moderation in all things."

We believe that tea is, in all truth, good for you. Beyond any of the medicinal benefits that are inherent in the plant's chemistry and physical composition, tea requires that its drinker take time to prepare and enjoy it. This five-minute ritual can provide a safe harbor in the rough seas of everyday living. Between kids, work, commuting, deadlines, grocery shopping, soccer games, and the like, this island of time for oneself can be crucial to both physical and mental well-being. If however, you are trying to gain the healthful benefits of tea from extracts, soap, candles, or other products that contain tea as an ingredient, the best we can say is we don't know if it is good for you. If you are taking enjoyment from the experience of the product, then it probably can't hurt you. If you are indulging somewhat obsessively we suggest that you take the time to brew a pot of dragon phoenix pearl jasmine, inhale deeply, and look in the Yellow Pages under psychologists.

Honestly, what are the scientific findings about tea? The news of tea's healthful benefits isn't making the front page of the *National Enquirer* next to alien babies and Elvis sightings, it's making headlines in the *New York Times*. The truth is, the scientific studies and their findings are constantly changing. Current research at some levels is plagued by conflicting and contradictory data, and is therefore difficult to translate into clear conclusions. The problem is not that the science is bad or inaccurate but that conclusions can only be drawn with complete confidence after long periods of research and study. Think of the research on tea and health as a Polaroid snapshot. It is still in the development stages and somewhat difficult to see clearly. With time, the image will develop into a clear and identifiable form. In the following section, we will try to make sense of some of the current research and what the likely implications are for tea and health, with the clear *caveat* that the story can and probably will change, and that, if scientific terminology bores you to tears, you might be crying by the end of this section. In other words, if you just don't care too much about things like polyphenols, catechins, and antioxidants, skip back to the tea recipes section and bake up a batch of scones. Goodness knows, we wouldn't blame you.

Scientific Studies on Tea

As a consumer, the first question you should ask is "Why all this excitement about tea?" The answer is that specific interest in tea as a healthy beverage has been prompted by more generalized studies pointing to the importance of maintaining a diet high in fruits and vegetables. One of the key benefits to a high vegetable intake is the relatively high levels of flavonoid compounds found in them. *Flavonoids* are a class of plant phenolics with recognized antioxidant properties. They are a nonnutritive substance with no observed vitamin function; a diet rich in fruits and vegetables can provide up to 1000 milligrams of flavonoids daily. Tea first caught the attention of researchers because of epidemiological studies showing significant differences in the occurences of certain types of cancers and heart disease between Asian and western peoples. Tea has continued to fascinate researchers because of its extraordinarily high flavonoid content—between 200 and 300 milligrams per cup! The major type of flavonoid found in tea is the catechin group, which constitutes 30 to 40 percent of the soluble makeup of green tea, and about 10 percent of black tea.

Stick with us here—we are about to throw in a number of initial sets and long names for the different catechins found in tea. There is no test following this chapter, and, unless you are conducting clinical research, you probably won't need to remember any of the names or initials, or even how to pronounce them. There are four principal catechins found in tea, and they have varying degrees of effectiveness as antioxidants. They are *Epigallocatechin gallate* (EGCG), *Epicatechin gallate* (ECG), *Epigallocatechin* (EGC), and *Epicatechin* (EC). The long names identify the different chemical structures involved, and make perfect sense to you . . . if you happen to be a biochemist. The only reason we even mention these names is to help you recognize them if you hear them bandied about in the latest round of media hysteria.

Tea polyphenols are thought to aid in cancer prevention through multiple mechanisms, and their antioxidant action is an important part of this protective role. Still, the scientific jury is out. In animal studies, they have been shown to be strongly effective as anticarcinogenic agents, but to date this has not been determined by human clinical studies. In fact, several large clinical intervention studies using the popular antioxidant supplement betacarotene have had disappointing results, and recently two U.S. studies were halted due to concerns over *increased* risk for cancer in study subjects taking these supplements.

Normally, studies on animals as well as humans are conducted using supplements that contain the desired agents in very high concentrations. This is yet another one of the reasons that interest in tea is so very high. Animal studies in mice and rats have shown good evidence for protective effect in a variety of different organs, with some showing a 50 percent reduction in cancer occurrence. Of special interest to scientists is that these animal studies were done with tea or its polyphenolic components administered in quantities that correspond to normal levels of human consumption. That is, consuming two to four cups of tea daily would provide polyphenols at the level as used in the very encouraging animal tests.

This reaffirms for us the real beauty of tea as a healthful beverage. You don't need to take a pill, drink an extract, or get a tea shot. Drinking tea, enjoying it as a beverage, provides you with, in a sense, medicinal levels of antioxidants! This is something rare, and does not seem to occur anywhere else in the vast spectrum of healthy foods, with the possible and notable exception of red wine.

Health Benefits

Besides the largest concern, cancer, current research points to some other possible benefits for tea. Some research is stronger than others, and none of it is 100 percent conclusive, but there are positive indications for scientists to perform more exacting controlled studies in the following areas.

Cardiovascular health—Tea may inhibit oxidation of LDL (low-density lipoproteins), which you may have heard referred to as *bad cholesterol*. Scientists believe that oxidized LDL is a potent initiator of coronary heart disease.

Antibacterial action—In vitro, or test-tube, studies show a well established action against *Staphylococcus aureas* and other species, again at levels provided by normal human consumption.

Healthy teeth—Both in vitro and *in vivo* (animal studies) show tea has a role in preventing dental caries, commonly known as cavities. Other studies show an inhibition of dental plaque formation. Tea is particularly rich in fluoride, an essential mineral for maintaining healthy teeth and bones.

Antimutagenic—In vitro studies show both green- and black-tea polyphenols inhibit the mutagenic action of a diverse group of carcinogens. That is, the seeds of cancer planted in DNA by carcinogens are blocked in every stage of their formation by catechins and other polyphenols found in tea.

What does it all mean to you, the tea consumer? Well, at the very least, there is an ongoing three-thousand-year-old epidemiological, or human observational, study that shows conclusively that drinking tea is not *bad* for you. In this day and age, there seem to be fewer and fewer things which we enjoy doing that are not somehow construed as being a health risk. On top of this, there is a large and growing body of scientific research that seems to indicate some very positive contributions to good health are made by drinking tea. We do, of course, hope that the results of this research will confirm that tea is a significant contributor to health, but, in the meantime, we advocate moderate consumption as an enjoyable and emotionally healthy pastime.

The Bottom Line on Caffeine

One of the most commonly asked questions about tea and health is in regard to caffeine content. Many people have concerns about the impact of caffeine and want to monitor their intake of this common stimulant. The question would seem to be a simple one: How much caffeine does tea contain? As in all things tea, the answer can be somewhat complicated.

Tea leaves typically contain from 3 to 5 percent caffeine by dry weight. This fails to provide a usable answer to the caffeine question, however, because no one sits down and eats a bowl of dry tea leaves. If they did, they would take in a massive amount of caffeine—nearly 15,000 milligrams for each pound consumed! Obviously, the real question is how much caffeine does the cup of tea I'm drinking contain? The answer, if given honestly, will always provide you with a range of caffeine milligrams.

Why isn't the answer a simple number? Caffeine content in the cup depends on the kind of tea you're drinking and how you prepare it. Caffeine is a molecule that is quite soluble in water. The amount of caffeine available to dissolve in water is dependent on the weight of dry tea used to brew a cup. Thus, if the traditional two grams of tea per 5.5 ounces of water brewing formula is used, the potential caffeine content for a cup of tea ranges from 60 to 100 milligrams. It doesn't stop here.

Although caffeine is soluble in water, the total caffeine present in a brewed cup of tea will be affected by both time and temperature. Hotter water causes caffeine to dissolve more quickly and thoroughly. A longer steeping time will extract more caffeine. Thus, we begin to see how brewing methods will influence caffeine content. The traditional method for brewing black tea calls for water just off the boil to be used to steep the tea for five minutes. By using this method, most black teas will yield 40 to 60 milligrams of caffeine per 5.5 ounce cup. Shorter brewing times or cooler water will yield slightly less. Beware! Lowering your water temperature and time will also get you a weaker, less flavorful cup of tea.

Traditional brewing instructions for green tea call for water at 180°F or less, and steeping times of two to three minutes. By following these instructions, a typical cup of green tea will contain from 15 to 30 milligrams of caffeine. Thus, while green tea is generally thought to contain less caffeine per cup, this is only true if it is brewed by traditional green tea methods.

Things are further complicated by the impact of leaf size and style on the whole process. Generally speaking, the larger the leaf, the slower the extraction of caffeine, due to the relatively low surface-to-weight ratio. This in part explains why oolong teas are generally regarded as producing cups with a caffeine content that is, like so many things oolong, somewhere in between black and green. Most oolong teas are produced with very large-leaf styles, as anyone who has examined the infused leaves of a good oolong tea can attest.

For a comparison of the relative caffeine content of teas and other beverages, see the chart on this page. Keep in mind the many factors that influence the final quantity of caffeine present in the cup, and consider how your tea-brewing habits will impact this.

What's in a Cup?

Coffee	
Drip	60–80 mg.
Instant	40–70 mg.
Tea (6 oz)	
Commercial brewed	20–80 mg.
Loose	
Black	25–110 mg.
Oolong	12–55 mg.
Green	8–36 mg.
Other (6 oz)	
Hot cocoa (6 oz)	2–20 mg.
Coca-Cola (12 oz.)	46 mg.

(*Source:* U.S. Food and Drug Administration)

Some Notes on Decaffeination

Perhaps after reading the preceding section, you are ready to give up and just go on to decaffeinated teas. If you drink decaffeinated teas because caffeine consumption bothers you, you may want to know a little bit more about how tea is decaffeinated.

Tea decaffeination is typically accomplished by one of two principal methods. Both use a natural solvent of sorts that has some affinity for bonding with the caffeine molecule. The first, ethyl acetate, uses a solution of ethyl acetate to extract caffeine, and the second, CO2, uses supercritical carbon dioxide. While both methods are relatively safe and effective, each has its benefits and drawbacks.

Ethyl acetate is a chemical compound that occurs naturally in a variety of edible plants and fruits, including, coincidentally, the tea plant. In reasonable doses it is nontoxic, and certainly to the degree in which it may appear in decaffeinated tea it does not present a health problem. From an effectiveness standpoint, ethyl acetate has a fair affinity for caffeine, and is both effective and reasonably cost-efficient. The major drawback to this form of decaffeination is the changes it brings to leaf appearance, and the effect it has on the overall flavor of the tea. This method typically imparts a distinctive fruity or sweet note to the tea. Additionally, because ethyl acetate is not as caffeine specific a solvent as other agents, it removes a larger quantity of other soluble materials, which also affects the quality of the cup.

Home Decaffeination

For the tea lover who is sensitive to caffeine at certain times, such as an after-dinner cuppa, or for those who just generally want to moderate caffeine intake, there is a simple method for partially decaffeinating just about any tea. The procedure is easy and fairly effective. Because caffeine is so easily dissolved in water, about 85 percent of the caffeine present in a cup of tea produced by traditional steeping methods will be dissolved in the brewing water in the first 45 to 60 seconds of steeping. You can take advantage of this to significantly lower the caffeine content in your cup of tea by using the following procedure.

1. Measure tea as you usually do into your customary pot or other brewing vessel. (Or simply place a tea bag into your favorite cup or mug.)
2. Pour the hot water you would normally prepare for steeping over the measured tea, and set your timer for one minute.
3. When the minute has expired, pour off the liquid and discard.
4. Heat fresh water to the appropriate temperature for the tea at hand, pour it over the wet

leaves left over from step 3, and allow to steep for the usual time (three to five minutes for most teas.)

5. Pour the resulting second infusion into a cup or mug and enjoy.

This simple process will yield teas with caffeine contents ranging from about 2.5 to 10 milligrams per cup, depending on the tea and the brewing parameters. However, like most other decaffeinated teas, there will be some loss of flavor and aroma.

The supercritical CO2 method is quite effective at removing caffeine, and has the added advantage of being taste and odor free. Additionally, CO2 is a completely innocuous molecule that makes up a substantial portion of the earth's atmosphere and, as such, represents no health risk whatsoever. This being the case, many CO2 decaffeinated teas carry a label reading "Naturally decaffeinated." The major disadvantage in this method is the enormous scale necessary to make this type of process economically viable. As a result, only teas which can be sold in *very* large quantities are typically used in this process (read commercial, lower grade tea here).

The decaffeination of black teas in general has a substantial impact on the flavor profile of the tea. Regardless of the process, many of the distinctive top notes and bright flavors are diminished, muddled, or altogether destroyed. Caffeine in black tea is involved chemically in the oxidation process, and is further involved in the creaming reaction that takes place in cooling brewed tea. Removing caffeine seems to cause some disruption of flavor. This disruption is less apparent in decaffeinated green teas, where the caffeine is not as significant as a flavor contributor. Decaffeinated green teas, while notably different, and generally somewhat muted relative to their unprocessed counterparts, tend to be closer in flavor to their antecedents than are decaffeinated black teas.

In either category, flavor changes are sufficient enough that most decaffeinated teas have natural and/or artificial flavors added after processing. Additionally, caffeine seems to enhance the perception of briskness in tea, and, therefore, only very bright black teas are truly excellent candidates for decaffeination, accounting for the relatively high percentage of Ceylons that are used for the process.

TEMPEST IN A TEAPOT

The tabloid headlines are screaming *Toxic Tea*! News anchors are standing outside foodservice establishments with serious expressions and wondering aloud if the super-sized iced tea you had at lunch will have you dead by dinner. Well, forget calling the mortuary and making arrangements, so far no one has died from drinking iced tea and, in fact, according to the

Center for Disease Control, there has been no identified case of any illness attributed to the consumption of iced tea.

What got the media excited was testing of food service beverages, which found a high concentration of microbiological activity in prepared iced tea. This took the form of CFUs (colony forming units) of *E. coli bacteria,* or fecal coliforms. This is the same nasty microorganism associated with the fatalities of a number of people from eating undercooked hamburgers. On the surface, this looked like another big story on a dangerous health risk.

In reality, poor testing methodology relevant to iced tea lead to the misidentification of a common bacteria, *Klebsiella,* as *E. coli.* These kinds of bacteria are common in many foods, especially leafy vegetables. The only concern, when all is said and done, is how well and how often tea dispensers are cleaned. Virtually every tea dispenser has a spigot for dispensing the tea into a glass or cup. Small amounts of tea are trapped within the spigot and, if the spigot is not properly cleaned, bacteria can flourish. The result is a vile smelling and tasting liquid which, I suppose, if consumed in any quantity, would probably cause symptoms similar to Montezuma's revenge. Fortunately, because of the very small quantity of liquid tea affected in the spigot, it's impossible to ingest a really significant amount.

The very simple solution is exactly the one that the tea industry recommended—clean tea dispensers thoroughly and daily. This not only reduces any health risk to essentially zero, but it also ensures that the tea in the dispenser will taste as good as it should. It also helps to remember that tea is food, and should be treated as such. Don't leave it out on the counter overnight. Left at room temperature for extended periods of time, brewed tea will grow bacteria. Refrigerate it for health, but for the best-tasting results, make it in small quantities and consume it all within a day or so. That said, sip your iced tea in peace.

The Future of Fine Tea

There is a pop song that says, "the future's so bright, I gotta wear shades," and there are many in the tea industry who are singing this tune. Truth is, we have been heralding the arrival of fine tea for close to a decade now. Whether by some happy accident of fate the trends we foresaw are finally coming to fruition or the industry just became tired of hearing about it: Tea is here! Americans aren't consuming any more tea, but they are consuming better and better teas. Before the celebration starts, here are some issues that should bear greater scrutiny by tea lovers and professionals.

The Demise of Orthodox Manufacture

In general, there are two available methods for processing tea—orthodox manufacture and CTC. Virtually all premium tea is made through orthodox manufacture, which is a batch process and consequently more time-consuming and expensive. CTC (crush, tear, and curl) is a more mechanized process, primarily used for the production of tea bag grades.

In the past decade, we have seen a huge increase in the use of CTC processing. All the commercial areas of interest, such as Kenya and Argentina are CTC, a fact that doesn't disturb too many tea lovers. More alarming is the fact that India, with the notable exception of the Darjeeling district (and a more recent interest in returning to traditional production methods in Assam), has given over almost entirely to CTC. Speculation has it that China would increase its use of this process exponentially but for the lack of initial capital to acquire the machinery.

The increase in CTC is due in large part to the fact that tea produced in this method yields more cups per kilo. Proof lies in the fact that tea consumption worldwide as measured by cups has increased tremendously in the past few years, while production figures have remained steady. Why? Because CTC doubles the cup per kilo yield. Furthermore, growers of tea have had to face harsh economic realities. CTC processing requires less time and labor, and produces teas that are acceptable to the majority of the market.

Make no mistake—this is not just a question of new technology replacing obsolete thinking and processes. CTC manufacture yields no leaf-grade teas. One of the great beauties of tea is in the seemingly endless variation in style that can be produced from the same plant. From hand-rolled Jasmine Pearls to the long, twisted leaves of Ceylon, orthodox manufacture is the mother of all that is unique in tea.

For true lovers of the leaf, this is an alarming trend. The only way to save orthodox manufacture and thus guarantee the future for fine teas, is to recognize the value of truly special teas. Consider the amount of human effort that goes into creating an essentially handmade premium tea. From the arduous business of cultivating tea plants, which occupy incredibly steep mountain terrain, to the Sisyphian task of plucking the fresh growth of the tea leaves by hand, to the critical and capital intensive processing and grading, every cup of good tea is the culmination of the efforts of literally hundreds of human beings. A Darjeeling plucker working on the steep slopes so common to the tea gardens of the area will spend an entire day plucking some 30,000 shoots, to produce what will eventually be a meager nine pounds of tea (see Fig. 9.1).

In the end, what is the cost to the consumer for this tremendous amount of care and effort? Well, the most outrageously expensive teas in the world might

Figure 9.1 Pickers make their way to the tea garden to begin a day's plucking.
(© Ambootia, Photographer: James Prinz, Chicago)

sell for something in the neighborhood of $300.00 per pound. With a yield of 200 cups per pound, this translates to a cost per cup of $1.50. Imagine this—the world's very best for $1.50 a cup! Suppose that you could buy the world's best wine for similar prices. This would have you paying $7.50 for a bottle of the world's great vintages. In reality, you cannot touch a well-regarded bottle of wine for twice this, much less the world's finest bottles, which can cost in the hundreds of dollars.

Resurgent interest in great tea is the only viable savior for the premium tea industry. On the positive side, tremendous European interest in specialty teas, and a growing interest in the U.S., are driving the premium market. Intense competition for an ever-dwindling supply of fine orthodox teas has had the effect of raising prices somewhat. More important, it has also encouraged some tea producers to continue traditional manufacturing, with an eye towards increasing quality rather than yield. It is our sincere hope that the American consumer in particular will discover the healthy joys of drinking great tea, and that a tradition many thousands of years old will continue to thrive.

Specialty Tea and Teahouses in the U.S.

It wasn't very long ago that, if you wanted to buy good tea, you were relegated to sight-unseen, mail-order purchases from some obscure vendor or, at best, hoping to find something at the local gourmet-foods store that was not more packaging than product. We do not mean to denigrate in any fashion the long-established mail-order houses who have been selling great teas for many years. Still, it is difficult to have a meaningful dialogue with the retailer in a mail-order scenario, and even more challenging to get a good sensory perception of the product before a purchase.

The rise of the specialty coffee trade in the United States saw the advent of a coffee retailer on nearly every street corner of every major city in the country. Many of them also carried tea in some form, as tea and coffee seem to be natural companions in the American retail landscape. Unfortunately, those few retailers who were doing a truly excellent job with coffee seldom had the time and energy to do a similarly good job with tea. Premium tea became a collection of stale, slow moving, poorly merchandised, and seldom-talked-about oddments gathering dust on the back shelves of coffee retailers across the nation. A very few companies, with longstanding interests in tea, promoted, cared for, and prized their tea programs.

There has been a tiny cadre of dedicated and passionate teahouse proprietors scattered across the urbanized United States for many years, and if one was a dedicated fan of tea, finding them was generally well worth the effort. Apart from this smattering of tiny vendors, the only other likely venue for taking tea outside the home was in fine hotels that frequently served an afternoon tea in the British tradition. Even here, the service was likely better than the tea itself. Slowly, quietly, in the very gentle manner typical of tea, this is changing. Teahouses in every possible style are proliferating. Tea is becoming widely available in loose form from a host of new vendors, and even the quality of tea bags is improving in better markets. So, what happened?

There is no single answer as to why tea is becoming increasingly popular. Certainly, some of it is the natural progression of the consumer interested in a wide range of gustatory experiences moving from coffee on to tea. A great deal of interest has been sparked by flashy reports on tea and health, with some new consumers breathing a sigh of relief that they can enjoy something so luxurious without risking their health, and maybe even improving it. An influx of Asian immigrants to the western United States has brought with it that integral part of their culture—the teahouse. Many established Asian concerns have opened retail outlets in this country to serve the needs of the immigrant community and are looking for ways to move out into the American mainstream. Certainly, the shrinking size of the planet, driven by ever faster communication and travel, has opened the market for new experiences, and other cultural perspectives.

Another driving force in the increasing enjoyment of tea is the lifestyle fatigue of the 1990s. From the early 1980s through today, our lives seem to be constantly accelerating. More and more vehicles for communication, from pagers to cellular phones to fax and e-mail, seem to have us working or running constantly. Coffee, the ultimate on the go beverage, fit nicely into this ever-more-hurried lifestyle. However, after 15 years or more of this frenetic pace, many Americans have started to search for ways to simplify their lives and look for refuge from the intense pressures of everyday living. Tea offers good solutions to all of these issues. By its very nature, it is a contemplative, soothing beverage. Rituals surrounding tea encourage taking time to stop, get centered, and let constant motion give way to thoughtful examination of the issues at hand. Add to this the guilt-free pleasure of indulging in this healthy, fascinating beverage, and the stage was set for growth in interest and consumption.

Whatever your pleasure in tea, from Victorian to Zen, some manifestation in the form of a tea house is almost certainly on its way to appearing near you. From a handful of generally urban locations as recently as ten years ago, there are now over 1000 teahouses across North America. New players are emerging constantly, and they bring with them enthusiasm, energy, and a fresh new outlook on tea.

There are many ways to find these rapidly appearing new ventures. Books cataloging them have been published, phone directories are adding them as a heading, and tea lovers and aficionados are spreading the word. Perhaps the most interesting and significant source for information on the subject is the increasingly more ubiquitous jungle drum of the late twentieth century, the Internet.

Tea and the Internet: The Misinformation Superhighway

First of all, let us make clear that we absolutely love the idea and, in many ways, the execution and the concept of cybercommunication. It is an endless source of interest, amazement, and delight to us, not only as tea people but as a tiny part of the world community. The Internet in some ways is the perfect venue for tea. It reaches a vast, participating audience, yet it can be accessed and enjoyed quietly and peacefully almost any time. Very tealike. There are a number of tea-oriented bulletin boards, news groups, e-mail lists, and so on, and a huge proliferation of commercial sites. Many new players in the tea market have begun as Internet and mail order ventures, and there are dozens and dozens of web pages presenting their products.

We are happy to see so much tea available, and so much interest about tea generated. Into all of this variety and interest, we would like to add a word of caution. Some of the tea information we have encountered is misleading, self-serving, or just plain wrong. We advocate looking at as many different sources for information as you can, and maintaining a healthy skepticism when you encounter conflicting positions.

If you are going to purchase tea through any of the Internet vendors, apply the same rules to rating them as you would any other retailer (see Chapter 5). Start an e-mail dialogue with them if possible, and find out what they know about their teas.

Organic Tea

Consumers are beginning to pay close attention to how agricultural products are grown and processed, and this has driven growth and interest in the organic movement worldwide. The European market, in particular, has focused intensely on this approach to farming, and many foods and beverages are becoming available with organic certification. In its infancy, organic often meant that quality was sacrificed at the altar of environmentally friendly farming, but that has changed dramatically in recent years. Organic tea has come to the United States amid varying degrees of welcome and controversy. We feel strongly that some of the issues surrounding this topic need to be addressed.

First of all, what does it mean to be organic? The average person will answer "grown without pesticides." While growing and processing food in a chemically free environment is a basic tenet of the organic movement, it is not the sole qualifier. Organic farming is at once a very complex and simple system of producing food. In its ideal representation, it produces products that adhere to strict standards addressing growth, harvesting, preservation, processing, storage, transportation, and marketing.

Human nature being what it is, truly organic products must be able to withstand close inspection, and there are a number of independent certification programs that undertake on-site farm inspections, publish standards, and mandate clear, traceable, audit trails, from farm to market. We would not presume to address all the issues involved with organic farming and products here, but strongly encourage the interested consumer to pursue more information on the topic.

As far as tea is concerned, we are happy to report that there is a growing community of dedicated organic producers, and they are growing, processing and marketing some products of exceptional quality. Beware the self-appointed expert who claims that virtually all tea is organically produced, although not certified. Certainly there are small farmers growing tea who cannot afford either pesticides and chemical fertilizers, much less organic certification, but they are a minority. While we won't claim that the *Fortune* magazine most-influential list is brimming with tea people and tea money, there are many growers who have a comfortable standard of living. Tea is a multibillion dollar industry, with players all over the world, and they include some of the most sophisticated and shrewd marketers and business people on the planet.

The dedicated organic tea growers who are currently producing certified organic teas have demon-

The Precepts of Organic Farming

An organic system means more than grown without pesticides; it encompasses a whole set of economic, social, and environmental ideologies. Organic is a complex system that

- Seeks to provide food of high nutritional value, using practices and materials that do not place human health at risk (see Fig. 9.2)
- Uses renewable resources to the greatest extent possible, within agricultural systems that are locally organized
- Maintains diversity within the farming system and in its surroundings, including the protection of plant and wildlife habitat
- Replenishes and maintains long-term soil fertility by providing optimal conditions for soil biological activity and health
- Provides livestock and poultry with conditions that meet both health and behavioral requirements, including particular concern for the ethological needs
- Minimizes all forms of environmental degradation that could result from activities associated with producing foods

(Source: Ambootia Tea Gardens)

Figure 9.2 A diverse selection of plant life and terraced slopes designed to prevent soil erosion are just a part of the conscientious practice of good farming techniques on this organic and biodynamic certified tea garden. (© Ambootia, Photographer: James Prinz, Chicago)

strated a commitment not only to environmentally sound farming practices, but also to the production of top quality teas. If these issues are important to you, be assured that these products are available, and more and more are coming to market.

APPENDIX A

Tea Tasting Terminology

Bakey: characteristic of an overfired black tea from which too much moisture has been removed.

Biscuity: a pleasant aroma often used to describe quality Assams.

Bright: a characteristic associated with good color, generally a signature characteristic of quality tea.

Brisk: another characteristic of well-manufactured, quality tea. Brisk denotes a live quality associated with pungency.

Common: a plain, thin liquor that has no distinct flavor characteristics.

Dull: refers to the liquid's color, the opposite of bright. A dull tea produces a cloudy brew. May also denote lack of briskness.

Flat: applies to tea that is no longer fresh, tastes like it sounds.

Full: describes a good combination of color and strength. May not indicate briskness, but denotes a round, smooth mouthfeel.

Hard: a pungent liquor related to greenness, accompanied by a harsh, bitter or rasping quality.

Harsh: describes a tea that has been underwithered, resulting in a very rough liquor.

Heavy: a thick, strong and darkly colored liquor with little life or briskness.

Light: liquor that lacks color and strength. Often this tea will lack body and aroma as well.

Malty: a desirable quality commonly found in Assam teas.

Metallic: a sharp, coppery flavor found in some black teas.

Muscat: a flavor and aroma characteristic of fine Darjeelings, often associated with black currants.

Pungent: a bitter, harsh, or rough characteristic that is felt along the gums rather than tasted on the tongue. (see also briskness)

Smoky: a characteristic flavor and aroma of some Chinese teas, especially Lapsang Souchong. May also be found in other teas, in which case it is quite undesirable, and usually results from leaks around the dryer heating tubes during processing.

Stale: faded aroma and a dead taste caused by excessive age and subsequent loss of quality.

Thin: light liquor lacking any strong or desirable characteristics.

Toasty: describes the aroma of a fine Keemun and other highly fired teas.

Weedy: grassy or haylike taste related to underwithering. May also refer to a woody taste. Green teas often have a distinct vegetal aroma and flavor.

Winy: relates to the aging of tea, which normally does not enhance flavor. In a fine Keemun or Darjeeling, however, aging may bring out a mellow characteristic.

APPENDIX B

Tea Resources

FINE TEAS: RETAIL & MAIL-ORDER

A Cuppa Tea Bar
116 Laidley Street
San Francisco, CA 94131

Akbar's Finest Teas
PO Box 353
Boise, ID 83701
Tea, teapots, infusers, gift baskets

Alpenglo Tea Co.
580 California Street, Suite 500
San Francisco, CA 94104

Angie's Special Teas & Accessories
PO Box 41335
Cleveland, OH 44141
Mail order, foods, gift products

Canada Creek Tea Merchants Inc.
286 North Aldershot Road
Kentville, Nova Scotia B4N 3V7 CANADA
Mail order

Carnelian Rose Tea Co.
14813 NE Salmon Creek Avenue
Vancouver, WA 98686-1618
Mail order

Coffee Tree
50 Greenwich Avenue
Greenwich, CT 06830

David Rio Coffee & Tea, Inc.
21 C Mirabel Avenue
San Francisco, CA 94110
Mail order

Everyone's Cup of Tea
837 5th Street
Santa Rosa, CA 95404
Etiquette consultant, tea, tea books, tea-related products

Freed, Teller & Freed
1326 Polk Street
San Francisco, CA 94109
Premium tea blending, wholesale/retail tea

Gerard's Coffee & Tea
N112W16278 Mequon Rd.
PO Box 637
Germantown, WI 53022

Gourmet Express
3000 Dundee Road, #302
Northbrook, IL 60062
Mail order, premium tea, teapots

Grace Tea Company
50 West 17th Street
New York, NY 10011
Packaged teas, orthodox teas, paper tea filters

Great Galena Peddlery (The)
116 N. Main Street
Galena, IL 61036
Tea and tea pots; Herbs and spices; Dried flowers, wreaths, and Arrangements

Harney & Sons
23 Brook Street
Lakeville, CT 06039
Tea, gift products

House of Coffee
1618 Noriega Street
San Francisco, CA 94122-4306
Coffee, retail and wholesale; Tea, retail and wholesale; coffee- and tea-related products; candies and gourmet products

Lisa's Tea Treasures
1145 Merrill Street
Menlo Park, CA 94025

Mark T. Wendell & Co.
50 Beharrel Street
West Concord, MA 01742
Mail order, wholesale bulk tea, wholesale packaged tea

Mission Valley Coffee Roasting Co.
40059 Mission Blvd.
Fremont, CA 94539-3680

Northshire Bookstore
PO Box 2200
Manchester Center, VT 05255

Peet's Coffee & Tea
1400 Park Avenue
Emeryville, CA 94608
Fine teas and coffees

Republic of Tea (The)
8 Digital Drive, Ste. 100
Novato, CA 94949 USA
Mail order

Royal Gardens Tea Company
19100 S. Harbor
Fort Bragg, CA 95437
Mail order, bulk tea, packaged tea

Serendipitea
Post Office Box 81
Ridgefield, CT 06877
Mail order; premium loose-leaf tea, packaged; premium loose-leaf tea, bulk; tea accouterments, wholesale

Silver Basket Co. & Tea Room
PO Box 522
Albany, Georgia 31702

Specialteas, Inc.
500 Summer Street, Suite 404
Stamford, CT 06901
Mail order, premium loose-leaf teas, fruit blends and herbals, tea accessories

Susan's Coffee & Tea
578 Kennedy Road
Akron, OH 44305

Takashimaya
693 Fifth Avenue
New York, NY 10022

Tea House on Los Rios (The)
31731 Los Rios Street
San Juan Capistrano, CA 92675

TeaSource
2900 Hayes St. N.E.
Minneapolis, MN 55418
Tea and tea accessories, retail and wholesale

Trident Booksellers & Café
940 Pearl Street
Boulder, CO 80302
Retailer/sit-down café, retail tea and coffee, small line of pastries

Universal Blends
1410 Kasold
Lawrence, KS 66049

Village Roaster
9255 W. Alameda
Lakewood, CO 80226

Wholesale Tea Merchants

ABC Tea House
14520 Arrow Highway
Baldwin Park, CA 91706
Wholesale bulk tea, wholesale packaged tea, tea packing and teabags, private label contract packing

Alexander Gourmet Imports
5630 Timberlea Blvd.
Mississauga, Ontario L4W 4M6 CANADA
Bulk and packaged teas, herbal teas, tea accessories, hot-cocoa mixes

Amber Tea Co. (The)
PO Box 1446
San Marcos, CA 92029–1446
Chai

Barnes & Watson Fine Teas
1319 Dexter Avenue N., Suite 30
Seattle, WA 98109

Berardi's Fresh Roast
12029 Abbey Road
Cleveland, OH 44133

Blue Willow Tea Company
911 E. Pike Street
Seattle, WA 98122
Loose-leaf teas in bulk packaging, loose-leaf teas in full chests, loose-leaf tea in retail packaging

Boyd Coffee Company
19730 N.E. Sandy Blvd.
Portland, OR 97230

Café Au Lait, Inc.
1111 Watson Center Drive, Suite A1
Carson, CA 90745
Paradise Tropical teas, Justin Lloyd teas

Café Moto
1205 J. Street
San Diego, CA 92101

Ceylon Teas Inc.
310 N. Palm Avenue, #B
Brea, CA 92821
Premium-quality flavored teas, tea gift items, private-label programs, therapeutic herbal and green teas

China Mist
7435 East Tierra Buena Lane
Scottsdale, AZ 85260
China Mist specialty teas, China Mist Tea-Loving Care

City & Country Fine Tea Co.
1809 130th Ave. NE, Suite #116
Bellevue, WA 98005

Wholesale bulk and packaged teas, wholesale teapots, wholesale tea accessories

Coffee Masters, Inc.
666 Russel Ct.
Woodstock, IL 60098

Continental Coffee Products
321 N. Clark Street, Suite 21-9
Chicago, IL 60610

Covington Coffee Works
228A N. Columbia Street
Covington, LA 70433

East India Tea & Coffee Co.
1933 Davis Street, Suite 308
San Leandro, CA 94577

Blended and varietal teas, loose; blended and varietal teas, bulk; blended prepackaged teabags; candies and cookies

East Indies Coffee & Tea
7 Keystone Drive
Lebanon, PA 17042

Gift products, packaged tea, bulk orthodox tea, private label

Frontier Coffee
PO Box 560
Urbana, IL 52345

Coffee, tea, herbs and spices, aromatherapy

GlobeTrends, Inc.
PO Box 461
Chatham, NJ 07928-0461
Taylor's of Harrogate, Telia tea filters

G. S. Haly Company, Inc. (The)
156 Arch Street
Redwood City, CA 94062
Wholesale tea, large quantity

Halssen & Lyon
Pickhuben No. 9
Hamburg, 20457 Germany

HTH Hamburger Teehandel GmbH
Am Sandtorkai 4/5, 2nd Floor
Hamburg, D-20457 Germany
Tea

Infinitea Foods, Inc.
PO Box 46022
Pointe Claire, Quebec H9R 5R4 Canada

J. G. British Imports
7933 Pinegrove Ct.
Sarasota, FL 34238

Leaves-Pure Teas
1392 Lowrie Avenue
S. San Francisco, CA 94080
Additive-free teas, pure teas; loose and bagged teas; tea bath; tea gifts, private label

Lindsay's Teas (Mountanos Bros. Coffee)
380 Swift Street, Suite 12
S. San Francisco, CA 94080

Teas, tisanes, infusions in canisters; bulk loose specialty tea; tea accessories and giftware; food-service iced tea and equipment

Mark T. Wendell & Co.
50 Beharrel Street
West Concord, MA 01742

Wholesale bulk tea, wholesale packaged tea

McKeany-Flavell Company, Inc.
11 Embarcadero West, Suite 200
Oakland, CA 94607

Private-label orthodox Indian teas, custom-blend quality Indian teas, flavored quality Indian teas

Neighbors Coffee & Tea
11 N.E. 11th Street
Oklahoma City, OK 73154

Qtrade International Corp.
13691 Gavina Avenue #480
Sylmar, CA 91342

Regal Tea
PO Box 492016
Los Angeles, CA 90049

Distributor, loose tea/tea bags

Republic of Tea (The)
750 South Hanley Road, Suite 40
Clayton, MO 63105

Roasterie, Inc. (The)
2601 Madison
Kansas City, MO 64108

Royal Coffee
PO Box 8542
Emeryville, CA 94662-0542
Green coffee importer, retail coffee and tea, wholesale coffee and tea

Royal Gardens Tea Company
19100 S. Harbor
Fort Bragg, CA 95437
Bulk tea, packaged tea

Serendipitea
Post Office Box 81
Ridgefield, CT 06877
Premium loose-leaf tea, packaged; premium loose-leaf tea, bulk; tea accouterments, wholesale

Southern Crown Tea Co.
8580 W. Washington Blvd.
Culver City, CA 90232

Stash Tea Company
PO Box 910
Portland, OR 97207

TAZO
PO Box 66
Portland, OR 97207

Uncle Lee's Tea, Inc.
11020 E. Rush Street
South El Monte, CA 91733

Wagner's Gourmet Foods
4500 North Chase Pkwy.
Wilmington, NC 28405

Water & Leaves
690 Broadway Street
Redwood City, CA 94063
Teas, teapots

Windward Trading Company
PO Box 9833
San Rafael, CA 94912
Coffee and tea accessories, bulk tea, permanent coffee and tea filters, coffee and tea preparation equipment

Xanadu (Coffee Bean Intl., Inc.)
2181 N.W. Nicolai
Portland, OR 97210
Xanadu bulk specialty tea; Xanadu packaged teas, loose in tins; Xanadu teabag teas in tins; Xanadu teas in foodservice rack

Xcell International Corp.
646 Blackhawk Drive
Westmont, IL 60559
Wholesale tea, tea-related smallware

PUBLICATIONS

Fancy Food
20 N. Wacker Drive, Suite 1865
Chicago, IL 60606

Fresh Cup
PO Box 82817
Portland, OR 97282-0817

Gourmet Retailer (The)
3301 Ponce De Leon Blvd., Suite 300
Coral Gables, FL 33134

Tea & Coffee Trade Journal
130 West 42nd Street, Suite 1050
New York, NY 10036

The Tea Quarterly
2118 Wilshire Blvd., #634
Santa Monica, CA 90403

Tea Talk
PO Box 860
Sausalito, CA 94966

TEA EXPERTS & CONSULTANTS

Business Development Labs, Inc.
825 W. Market Street
Salinas, CA 95039

Contract packaging, product development, milling and blending

Illahe Hills Tea Farms
1050 District Line Road
Burlington, WA 98233
Research, Agricultural Consulting

Industrial Laboratories
1450 E. 62nd Avenue
Denver, CO 80216
Research/analysis

James Norwood Pratt
828 Green
San Francisco, CA 94133
Professional speaker, consultant, tea wit and wisdom

Paragon Packaging
49B Sherwood Terrace
Lake Bluff, IL 60044
Gourmet packaging, packaging consulting

R2 Consultants
10842 Noel St., Suite 107
Los Alamitos, CA 90720
Product development, marketing and research, production/process consulting, small-batch custom tea and coffee, blending

Sage Group
1712 Warren Avenue North
Seattle, WA 98109

"U.S. Tea Is Hot" report, Tea products research and development, market research, business planning

Twentyman Tea & Coffee
RR 1, Site 10, Comp 4
Garden Bay, BC V0N 1S0 Canada

Related Services

Café Away
PO Box 61482
Denver, CO 80206
Tea-related travel

Cricklewood Cottage
4182 Chasin Street
Oceanside, CA 92056
Wholesale custom tea cozies

Edgecraft Corporation
825 Southwood Road
Avondale, PA 19311
Chef's Choice International TeaMate TeaMaker, Chef's Choice International Deluxe Electric Teakettle

Water System Group (The)
5312 Derry Avenue, #A
Agoura Hills, CA 91301
Complete line of water-treatment equipment, consulting for specialty water formulations,

maintenance programs for water-treatment systems

Commercial Equipment

Affinitea Brewing Technologies
318 Pleasant Street
Roseville, CA 95678

AquaBrew, Inc.
3421 Fordham Avenue
Santa Ana, CA 92704

Bunn-O-Matic
1400 Stevenson Drive
Springfield, IL 62703
Tea brewers and dispensers

IMA North America, Inc.
418 Meadow Street
Fairfield, CT 06460
Tea-packaging equipment, end-of-line equipment

Wilbur Curtis Co., Inc.
1781 N. Indiana
Los Angeles, CA 90063
Commercial tea-brewing equipment, iced-tea equipment, hot-tea water towers, tea dispensers

Select Bibliography

Bersten, Ian. *Coffee Floats, Tea Sinks*. Roseville, Australia: Helian Books, 1993

Chow, Kit, and Kramer, Ione. *All The Tea In China.* San Francisco: China Books, 1990

McCoy, Elin and Walker, John F. *Coffee and Tea.* New York: Raines & Raines, 1991

Okakura, Kakuzo. *The Book of Tea.* New York: Dover Publications, Inc. 1964

Pratt, James Norwood. *Tea Lovers' Treasury.* Santa Rosa, CA: Cole Group, 1982

Sen, Soshitsu. *Tea Life, Tea Mind.* New York: John Weatherhill, 1981

Stella, Alain, et al. *The Book of Tea.* Paris, France: Flammarion, 1992

Ukers, William H. *All About Tea.* New York: Tea & Coffee Trade Journal Company, 1935

Wilson, K. C., and Clifford, M. N., eds. *Tea, Cultivation to Consumption.* New York: Chapman & Hall, 1992

INDEX